CW00509085

Allāh and His angels send blessings on the Prophet: O you who believe! Send blessings on him, and salute him with all respect

(Qur'ān 33:56)

Ṣalāt & Salām

In Praise of Allāh's Most Beloved

محمد رسول الله

Ṣalāt & Salām

In Praise of Allāh's Most Beloved

A MANUAL OF BLESSINGS & PEACE ON
THE PROPHET MUḤAMMAD ﷺ

Based on the works of Shaykh Muḥammad ibn ʿAbd al-Raḥmān al-Sakhāwī, Shaykh Ashraf ʿAlī Thānawī, Shaykh Yusuf ibn Sulayman Motala, and Makhdūm Muḥammad Sindhī

Compiled and Translated with an Introduction by
ABDUR-RAHMAN IBN YUSUF MANGERA

First Edition November 2007 Reprint 2009, 2012, 2016 and July 2018

ISBN: 978-1-933764-02-3 (softcover), 978-1-933764-04-7 (hardcover)

Published by:
White Thread Press
White Thread Limited, London, UK
www.whitethreadpress.com

Distributed in the UK by Azhar Academy Ltd. London
www.azharacademy.com

Library of Congress Cataloging-in-Publication Data

Salat & salam : in praise of Allah's most beloved : a manual of blessings & salutations on the prophet Muhammad ﷺ: from the collections of Muhammad ibn 'Abd al-Rahman al-Sakhawi, Shaykh Ashraf 'Ali Thanawi, Shaykh Yusuf ibn Sulayman Motala, and Makhdum Muhammad Sindhi / compiled and translated with an Introduction by Abdur-Rahman ibn Yusuf. – 1st ed.

p. cm.

Includes bibliographical references.

ISBN-13: 978-1-933764-04-7 (hardback: alk. paper) ISBN-10: 1-933764-04-X (hardback: alk. paper) ISBN-13: 978-1-933764-02-3 (pbk.: alk. paper) ISBN-10: 1-933764-02-3 (pbk.: alk. paper)

1. Muhammad, Prophet, d. 632–Devotional literature. 2. Islam–Prayers and devotions. I. Sakhawi, Muhammad ibn 'Abd al-Rahman, 1427 or 8-1497. II. Ibn Yusuf, Abdur-Rahman, 1974- III. Title: Salat and salam. BP76.2.S356 2007
297.3'824–dc22

2007029103

Cover design by Abdallatif Whiteman
Book design and typography by ARM

♾ Printed and bound in the United States of America on premium acid-free paper.

For My Beloved Parents

Transliteration Key

ء (أ إ)	ʾ (A slight catch in the breath. It is also used to indicate where the *hamza* has been dropped from the beginning of a word.)
ا	a, ā
ب	b
ت	t
ث	th (Should be pronounced as the *th* in *thin* or *thirst*.)
ج	j
ح	ḥ (Tensely breathed *h* sound.)
خ	kh (Pronounced like the *ch* in Scottish *loch* with the mouth hollowed to produce a full sound.)
د	d
ذ	dh (Should be pronounced as the *th* in *this* or *that*.)
ر	r
ز	z
س	s
ش	sh
ص	ṣ (A heavy *s* pronounced far back in the mouth with the mouth hollowed to produce a full sound.)
ض	ḍ (A heavy *d/dh* pronounced far back in the mouth with the mouth hollowed to produce a full sound.)
ط	ṭ (A heavy *t* pronounced far back in the mouth with the mouth hollowed to produce a full sound.)
ظ	ẓ (A heavy *dh* pronounced far back in the mouth with the mouth hollowed to produce a full sound.)
ع	ʿ, ʿa, ʿi, ʿu (Pronounced from the throat.)
غ	gh (Pronounced like a throaty French *r* with the mouth hollowed to produce a full sound.)
ف	f
ق	q (A guttural *q* sound with the mouth hollowed to produce a full sound.)
ك	k
ل	l
م	m
ن	n
و	w, ū, u.
ه	h
ي	y, ī, i
ﷺ	Used following the mention of the Messenger Muḥammad, translated as, "May Allāh bless him and give him peace."
﵇	Used following the mention of a Prophet or Messenger of Allāh, translated as, "May the peace of Allāh be upon him."
﵁	Used following the mention of a Companion of the Messenger, translated as, "May Allāh be pleased with him."
﵃	Used following the mention of more than one Companion of the Messenger (and also after a female Companion in this work), translated as, "May Allāh be pleased with them."

The *duʿās* in this book have been transliterated using a convention different from the standard used for transliterating Arabic terms in the main text. Hence, words are represented as they should be pronounced and the interword connections are transliterated according to the following guidelines:

(1) Silent *hamzas* (*waṣl*) have been omitted and replaced with an apostrophe ('). In this case, the word before it should be connected to the letter after the apostrophe; e.g., *wa 'l-māli.*

(2) Commas have been added to indicate appropriate places of pause. Letters enclosed in parentheses are not read when pausing; e.g., *fī khayr(in).*

(3) In instances where there is elision (*idgham*) between two words, the words are transliterated in their elided forms; e.g., *wāsi-ʿaw wa shifā'am min.* However, in some cases, to facilitate a pause, the non-elided form is shown, followed by the elided form in square brackets; e.g., *jadīdan[w], wa.* In this example, the [*w*] replaces *n* only when continuing.

Contents

⁕

In the name of Allāh
Most Gracious, Most Merciful

All praise is to Allāh who raised the mention of His beloved in the worlds, and blessings and peace be upon the leader of those who have gone and those to come, our Master, Muḥammad, the intercessor for the sinful, and blessings upon his family, Companions, and upon those who have followed his path

Introduction

⁂

When a physician treats us for a broken bone, we express our gratitude. When a lawyer successfully advocates on our behalf, we express our gratitude. We feel obliged to thank such people, despite the absence of any personal relationship with them. It may have been nothing more than one of their professional obligations, and yet we are grateful to them, regardless of their motives or intentions. An Arabic proverb holds that "Man is a slave to favors."

It is natural for us to feel obliged toward those who benefit us in some way or another, and there is no denying that the greatest source of blessing and mercy for the Muslim and for all of mankind is Muḥammad, the beloved Messenger of Allāh ﷺ. He was sent by Allāh as the Mercy of the Worlds, and was chosen by Him as the final prophet to guide mankind to His path. The sacrifices he made are not lost on his Umma, as there are many books and sermons replete with references to them. Muslims, the most privileged recipients of this source of mercy, are required to invoke blessings (*ṣalāt*) on the Messenger of Allāh ﷺ. Therefore, invoking blessings upon him is more than just a demand of altruism; it is incumbent upon us as an expression of our loyalty to him. His favors and generosity upon us are more than can be enumerated, and as such, we are eternally grateful and indebted to him ﷺ for his efforts in calling humanity to the straight path, thereby attaining everlasting felicity.

Unlike praising others, invoking blessings on the Messenger of Allāh ﷺ holds great reward for the suppliant. The Messenger ﷺ said, "Whoever sends one blessing upon me, Allāh will send ten blessings upon him" (*Muslim*). Therefore, even though we may not be inherently altruistic, doing this simply for our own benefit is still highly desirable. Abū Muḥammad al-Marjānī says, "Your invoking blessings upon him is, in reality, praying for yourself, since the benefits of it are returning to you" (*Al-Qawl al-Badīʿ* 83). Sending blessings upon him firmly establishes love for him in one's heart, causing it to improve and expand. Love for him is one of the necessary components of faith, without which it remains incomplete. The more a servant remembers him, evokes his presence in his heart, and recalls his beautiful characteristics and qualities, the more his love and longing for him will grow, until it fills the expanse of his heart. ʿAbdullāh ibn Masʿūd ﷺ relates that the Messenger of Allāh ﷺ said, "The closest to me on the Day of Judgment will be the one who invokes blessings upon me most abundantly" (*Tirmidhī*). Many other benefits of sending blessings upon the Prophet ﷺ have been explained in the sacred sources and from the personal experiences of the scholars and saints. The ḥadīth master Shams al-Dīn al-Sakhāwī (d. 902/1496) mentions a number of these benefits in his *Al-Qawl al-Badīʿ fi 'l-Ṣalāt ʿala 'l-Ḥabīb al-Shafiʿ* (The Eloquent Word Concerning the Blessings on the Beloved Intercessor), some of which are provided below:

> Allāh, His angels, and His Messenger send mercy on the one who invokes blessings. Such a person's wrongdoings are expiated, his good deeds increased and purified, and his status elevated. The blessings [themselves] seek forgiveness for him and his sins are forgiven. A *qīrāṭ* [measure equivalent to Mount Uhud] of reward is allotted for him. His rewards are weighed by a perfect scale on the Day of Judgment. For whoever makes it his complete regimen by day and night, both his worldly and otherworldly matters are taken care of, and his wrongdoings are wiped away. It is superior to freeing slaves and a source of protection from turmoil on the Day of Judgment. The Messenger of Allāh ﷺ will testify on his behalf on the Day of Judgment, and his intercession will be guaranteed for him. He will be protected from the wrath of Allāh, gain a place in the shade of the Throne of Allāh, and the pan of his good deeds will be heavier in the Scale. He will be honored with presence at the watering place (*ḥawḍ*), protected from thirst on the Day of Judgment, and will cross the bridge with speed. He is shown his abode in Paradise before his death, his wealth is increased, and more than a hundred needs of his are fulfilled. Sending blessings is the adornment of a gathering. It removes the hardships of poverty, and the suppliant gains closeness to the Messenger of Allāh ﷺ. Not only does the suppliant benefit through this act, but so does his progeny. It provides assistance against his enemies, purifies the heart from hypocrisy and rust,

> and generates love for him in the hearts of others. One of the greatest and most noble of benefits is that he sees the Messenger of Allāh ﷺ in a dream. It is one of those actions that are considered to be the most blessed, exalted, and beneficial for one's *dīn* and worldly existence (see pp. 231–232).

A more direct ḥadīth is related from Ubayy ibn Kaʿb ؓ. He says, "I asked, 'O Messenger of Allāh, I would like to increase my prayers for blessings upon you. How much of my invocations should I devote to this?' He replied, 'As much as you like.' I asked, 'One quarter?' He said, 'As much as you like, but the more you do, the better it is for you.' I asked, 'One half?' He said, 'As much as you like, but the more you do, the better it is for you.' So I said, 'Two thirds then?' He said, 'As much as you like, but the more you do, the better it is for you.' So I said, 'I will devote my entire time of invocation for you.' To this he ﷺ said, 'Then your concerns will all be taken care of and your sins will be forgiven'" (*Tirmidhī*).

Shaykh Muḥammad Manẓūr Nuʿmānī explains that Ubayy ibn Kaʿb ؓ, who was given to supplication, decided one day to allocate a portion of his time to praying for blessings upon the Messenger of Allāh ﷺ, so he asked the Messenger ﷺ how much time he should dedicate to it. He ﷺ did not stipulate any amount for him and left it to his discretion, although he did encourage him to do it abundantly. When Ubayy ؓ told him that he would spend his entire time of supplication doing it, he ﷺ gave him glad tidings. This is similar to what has been related by the Messenger of Allāh ﷺ in a ḥadīth qudsī in which Allāh says, "Whoever the Qur'ān occupies from remembering Me and beseeching Me, I will bestow upon him the best of what I bestow upon those who ask" (*Tirmidhī, Dāramī*). Whoever makes his entire daily regimen the recitation of the Qur'ān, and this occupies him from engaging in any other form of remembrance or supplication, Allāh will give him a superior reward. Similarly, here, Allāh will take care of all the needs of the one who has designated all of his supplication to Allāh's Beloved ﷺ (*Maʿārif al-Ḥadīth* 5:371–374, *Al-Qawl al-Badīʿ* 256, 287). Although the recitation of the Qur'ān comprises supplication and remembrance, what is essentially happening in both cases is that the person, in devoting his entire time to these acts, is expressing his reliance (*tawakkul*) on Allāh and his love and connection to Him and His Messenger, and is trusting in Allāh to take care of his needs. This involves a very high form of reliance on Him. Allāh takes care of the affairs of such people and gives them the best of rewards.

Invoking blessings is a worship that is presented to the Messenger of Allāh ﷺ in his grave. He ﷺ said, "Whoever sends blessings on me at my grave, I will hear it, and whoever sends blessings upon me away from it, it will be conveyed to me" (Bayhaqī, *Shuʿab al-Īmān*). In fact, our general supplications have a greater chance of being accepted by Allāh when they are accompanied by blessings on His Messenger ﷺ. ʿUmar ibn al-Khaṭṭāb ؓ relates that the Messenger of Allāh ﷺ said, "Verily supplication is suspended between the heavens and earth, and it does not ascend [to the heavens] until you send blessings upon your Prophet" (*Tirmidhī*). Abū Sulaymān al-Dārānī says, "Invoke blessings at the beginning and end of your supplications. Allāh is sure to accept both blessings and it is unlikely that Allāh will not accept what is in between" (*Zād al-Saʿīd* 27).

Numerous incidents have been related regarding the *baraka* gained by sending blessings upon the Messenger of Allāh ﷺ. Unfortunately, it is beyond the scope of this short manual to mention them all, so we will mention only a few. Fākihānī relates in his *Al-Fajr al-Munīr* that the pious Shaykh Ṣāliḥ Mūsā al-Ḍarīr related to him an incident. He said, "We were once at sea in a ship when a storm known as the *Iqlābiyya* (the upturning storm) brewed up; very few people have been saved from such a storm. I was suddenly overwhelmed by slumber and saw the Messenger of Allāh ﷺ teaching me an invocation (invocation 49 in this manual). He instructed that those on board the ship should read it one thousand times. We had not yet reached three hundred when Allāh delivered us from the calamity and the vessel was saved" (*Al-Qawl al-Badīʿ* 415). The reason behind the compilation of the famous manual *Dalā'il al-Khayrāt* (The Waymarks of Benefits) is also well known. The author Muḥammad ibn Sulaymān al-Jazūlī was in need of water to make *wuḍū'* during a journey. He was by a well, but there was no rope or pail in sight. A girl saw him in this state of despair and, after inquiring about his problem, spat into the well. The water suddenly rose to the surface and Jazūlī, astonished, made *wuḍū'* and asked her how she had reached such a rank. She told him that it was from the *baraka* of invoking blessings upon the Messenger of Allāh ﷺ. This inspired him to compile the famous manual *Dalā'il al-Khayrāt.*

Scholars have related many experiences in regard to seeing the Messenger of Allāh ﷺ in their dreams and have shared with us which invocations for blessings upon him ﷺ are most effective in achieving this. Sakhāwī states that it has been related that whoever desires to see the Prophet ﷺ in their dream should read the following an odd number of times:

اَللّٰهُمَّ صَلِّ عَلٰى مُحَمَّدٍ كَمَا أَمَرْتَنَا أَن نُّصَلِّيَ عَلَيْهِ، اَللّٰهُمَّ صَلِّ عَلٰى مُحَمَّدٍ كَمَا هُوَ أَهْلُهُ،
اَللّٰهُمَّ صَلِّ عَلٰى مُحَمَّدٍ كَمَا تُحِبُّ وَتَرْضٰى لَهُ

O Allāh, bless Muḥammad as You have commanded us to bless him;
O Allāh, bless Muḥammad as much as he is deserving [of that blessing];
O Allāh, bless Muḥammad as much as Your love and good pleasure for him.

To this one should also add:

اَللّٰهُمَّ صَلِّ عَلٰى رُوْحِ مُحَمَّدٍ فِي الْأَرْوَاحِ، وَصَلِّ عَلٰى جَسَدِ مُحَمَّدٍ فِي الْأَجْسَادِ،
وَصَلِّ عَلٰى قَبْرِ مُحَمَّدٍ فِي الْقُبُوْرِ

O Allāh, bless the spirit of Muḥammad among the spirits, bless the body of Muḥammad among the bodies, and bless the grave of Muḥammad among the graves (*Al-Qawl al-Badī*ʿ 282).

However, it should be borne in mind that this vision is not acquired by acts alone but is granted by Allāh to whom He wills.

The Definition of Ṣalāt and Salām

Allāh says, "Allāh and His angels send blessings on the Prophet: O you who believe! Send blessings upon him, and salute him with all respect" (Qur'ān 33:56). Allāh expresses the status accorded to the Prophet ﷺ by Him in the Higher Assembly; that He praises him in the presence of the intimate angels and that they also invoke blessings upon him. He then commands the inhabitants of the Lower Assembly to also invoke blessings and peace upon him. Therefore, blessings are invoked upon him throughout by the inhabitants of both the Upper and Lower Assemblies. Allāh commands two things in this verse: one is to send *ṣalāt* and the other is *salām*. With respect to *ṣalāt* (blessings), He says it is something that Allāh and His angels do, and so we should do it too. No doubt, what is meant by Allāh sending *ṣalāt* has to be different from our sending *ṣalāt* and also from how the angels send *ṣalāt*. Shaykh Muḥammad Manẓūr Nuʿmānī explains that the meaning of the word *ṣalāt* [in this context] will change according to who it is being attributed to. Hence *ṣalāt* from Allāh is His sending His blessings on His Messenger ﷺ, and when it comes from the angels and others, it is their praying to Allāh to send His blessings. The term *ṣalāt*, however, encompasses many meanings, such as honoring (*takrīm*), ennobling (*tashrīf*), praising (*madḥ*), elevating one's status, love, compassion, blessing, mercy, intending good, and praying for good. This same interpretation of the term *ṣalāt* thus can be attributed to Allāh, His angels, and His servants, the only difference being that *ṣalāt* made by Allāh would be in accordance with His High

Status and Power, and the angels and created beings in accordance to theirs. Therefore, the verse means that Allāh Most High loves and blesses His Messenger ﷺ, treats him with compassion, showers him with His mercy, honors, ennobles, and praises him, elevates his status, and bestows upon him His favors. The angels also love, honor, ennoble, and praise him, and entreat Allāh to raise his status, bless him, and shower him with his mercy. So, O believers, love, honor, ennoble, and praise him, and entreat Allāh to raise his status to the praiseworthy station, accept his intercession, and shower him with His mercy and blessings (*Maʿārif al-Ḥadīth* 5:354–355).

The second command in this verse is to send *salām* on the Prophet ﷺ. This means to invoke peace and safety for him, to pray that he and his message and his umma remain free of calamities and defects (*Al-Qawl al-Badīʿ* 162).

Finally, the reason we are commanded to ask Allāh to send blessings and peace on him, as opposed to doing it ourselves, is as quoted by Sakhāwī from Marghīnānī: "Because he is the pure one, without blemish, and we are with flaws and blemishes. So how can the one with flaws praise the one without? Therefore, we ask Allāh to send blessings on him so that the blessings are from the Pure Lord upon the Pure Prophet" (*Al-Qawl al-Badīʿ* 155).

Books and Manuals of Sending Blessings

Many books and manuals have been compiled which elaborate various ways of invoking peace and blessings upon the Prophet ﷺ. The most superior formulations are those which were recommended and related by the Messenger of Allāh ﷺ himself, among which is the *Ṣalāt Ibrāhīmiyya,* which is recited in the final sitting of the ritual prayers. However, there are many profound invocations formulated by scholars and saints like Ḥasan al-Baṣrī, ʿUmar ibn ʿAbd al-ʿAzīz, Sufyān ibn ʿUyayna, Zayn al-ʿĀbidīn ʿAlī ibn al-Ḥusayn, and Imām Shāfiʿī (may Allāh have mercy on them all), which contain very personal, deep, and eloquent meanings. Some of the more popular works and manuals on this subject are Shams al-Dīn al-Sakhāwī's *Al-Qawl al-Badīʿ fi 'l-Ṣalāt ʿala 'l-Ḥabīb al-Shafīʿ* (this has been considered a compendium on the subject), Abū ʿAbdillāh al-Numayrī al-Mālikī's *Kitāb al-Iʿlām bi Faḍl al-Ṣalāt ʿala 'l-Nabiyyi ʿalayhi Afḍal al-Ṣalāt wa 'l-Salām,* Abu 'l-Qāsim ibn Bashkuwāl's *Kitāb al-Qurba ilā Rabb al-ʿĀlamīn bi 'l-Ṣalāt ʿalā Muḥammad Sayyid al-Murasalīn Ṣallallāhu Taʿālā ʿalayhi wa ʿalā Ālihī wa Ṣaḥbihī Ajmaʿīn,* Ibn al-Qayyim al-Jawziyya's *Jilā' al-Afhām bi Ṣalāt al-Nabiyyi ʿalayhi 'l-Ṣalāt wa 'l-Salām,* and Muḥammad ibn Sulaymān al-Jazūlī's *Dalā'il al-Khayrāt.* Other scholars who have written on the subject include Majd al-Dīn al-Fayrūzābādī, Abu 'l-Shaykh Ibn Ḥayyān, Abu 'l-Fatḥ Ibn Sayyid al-Nās al-Yaʿmurī, Muḥibb al-Dīn al-Ṭabarī, and more recently Shaykh Ashraf ʿAlī Thānawī, Shaykh Zakariyya Khandhlawī, and Shaykh Muḥammad ibn al-ʿAlawī al-Mālikī. Reciting blessings on the Prophet ﷺ has come to represent an important part of many people's daily routine because of the blessing, mercy, and contentment that descends upon and inundates them, their families, and their homes. As such, many scholars and laypersons have felt greatly honored and obliged to compile, publish, and republish manuals and make them available to the masses.

The Ṣalawāt in This Manual

Part one consists of a collection of fifty invocations for blessings and peace upon the Messenger of Allāh ﷺ, of which the first forty were compiled from the ḥadīths by Ḥakīm al-Umma Mawlānā Ashraf ʿAlī Thānawī in his *Zād al-Saʿīd* (Provision for the Fortunate). The first twenty-five of these mainly consist of the different versions of the *Ṣalāt Ibrāhīmiyya*. These are followed by fifteen invocations for mercy (*salām*), mainly consisting of the different versions of *tashahhud* related in the ḥadīths. Shaykh Thānawī states that they are all *marfūʿ* narrations from the Messenger of Allāh ﷺ himself. Though a few seem to originate from a Companion, he states that they are most likely also learned from the Messenger ﷺ himself. Hence, it makes them *marfūʿ* as well (*marfūʿ ḥukmī*). This collection by Ḥakīm al-Umma became more well-known through Shaykh Zakariyya Kāndhlawī's *Faḍā'il Durūd Sharīf* (Virtues of the Noble Ṣalāt) in which they were quoted, and then even more so through being published independently in the form of small booklets by Ṣūfī Muḥammad Iqbāl of Madīna al-Munawwara, after which they have been distributed in the thousands by various individuals and organizations. It is a graceful and lucid collection that has been read the world over for decades.

An additional ten invocations have been added to the forty to complete this part. They have been specially selected for their richness, profundity, and excellence from ʿAllāma Makhdūm Muḥammad Hāshim Sindhī's *Dharīʿat al-Wuṣūl ilā Janāb al-Rasūl* ﷺ (The Means of Reaching the Presence of the Messenger ﷺ), which is essentially a compilation of various blessings from earlier books on the subject, and Sakhāwī's *Al-Qawl al-Badīʿ*, to which reference has also been provided after every narration.

Part two of the manual consists of brief invocations featuring the Ninety-Nine Names of Allāh Most High, coupled with the attributes of His beloved Messenger ﷺ. They were compiled and composed by our beloved Shaykh Mawlānā Yusuf ibn Sulayman Motala, the rector and Shaykh al-Ḥadīth of Darul Uloom, Bury, UK. He explains in his introduction that there are relatively few invocations transmitted by the Companions; many more have been composed by people who came later. Among them one will find many rhyming invocations, which contribute to a smoother recital and ease of memorization, and thus they are read with great interest and pleasure. In this collection, the shaykh has coupled with each one of the Ninety-Nine Names of Allāh, an attribute of Allāh's Messenger ﷺ. More than sixty of these Names were taken from Sakhāwī's *Al-Qawl al-Badīʿ* and the remainder from other sources. Wherever a matching attribute could not be found, he abandoned the scale in that invocation and used another related attribute. There are many benefits to this collection: one will receive the reward and blessings of both sending *ṣalāt* and reciting the names of Allāh; the Names of Allāh will become easier to memorize, regarding which the Messenger of Allāh ﷺ has said, "Allāh has Ninety-Nine Names. Whoever memorizes them will enter Paradise"; and by frequently repeating the names of His Messenger ﷺ, his love and respect will settle into one's heart.

In this collection, readers will notice that some of the names used in the Arabic for the Messenger of Allāh ﷺ are the same as those used for Allāh Most High. The shaykh explains that this should not be taken as a form of polytheism, since names like Ra'ūf (Compassionate, Kind) and Raḥīm (Most Merciful), which are among the Ninety-Nine Names of Allāh, have also been used for His Messenger ﷺ in the Qur'ān. For instance, Allāh says, "To the Believers is he [i.e., the Messenger] most kind and merciful" (Qur'ān 9:128). When names and qualities are attributed to Allāh, they are considered to be His essential qualities and transcendently complete and perfect, whereas when they are attributed to created beings, they are but the limited and imperfect qualities which Allāh has generously created for them (see introduction to *Ṣalāt wa Salām ʿalā Sayyid al-Anām* by Shaykh Yusuf Motala).

All the invocations in this manual have been translated afresh and are not revisions of any existing translations. For convenient, uninterrupted reading, the Arabic invocations have been placed on one side with their English translation on the facing side. A transliteration of all the invocations has been included for those who have difficulty reading the Arabic text. The purpose of this collection is to provide an elegant set of invocations for sending blessings upon Allāh's Most Beloved ﷺ, in which the words are rich and beautiful. Our aim is not to prove by them any legal matter or tenet of belief, but to present them for their sound invocational value. Therefore, even though the majority of the narrations are transmitted through strong chains, a few are from weaker sources. Detailed references have been cited for each prayer at the end of the work along with some of the benefits and virtues transmitted regarding some of the invocations. Most of the citations for the first forty ḥadīths have been taken from *Zād al-Saʿīd* and the separately published manuals. However, many of these have been verified and supplemented from other references that were found in *Al-Qawl al-Badīʿ* and other sources as have the citations for the remaining ten. Those who are interested in learning about the virtues of these prayers or want more details on their chains of transmissions can consult the source books from whence they were extracted.

When to Read This Manual

There is no fixed time to read this manual. The prayers can be read, for example, before or after the Fajr and Maghrib prayers, before reading the Qur'ān, or before beseeching Allāh for any need. There are many virtues mentioned in the ḥadīths regarding sending blessings on Friday nights in particular (that is, the night between Thursday and Friday). Aws ibn Aws ؓ relates that the Messenger of Allāh ﷺ said,

"The best of your days is Friday, so send blessings abundantly upon me this day, for your blessings are presented to me." The Companions asked, "How will they be presented to you when you have disintegrated?" He replied, "Verily Allāh has made the bodies of prophets unlawful to the earth" (*Abū Dāwūd, Nasā'ī, Ibn Māja*). Therefore, in accordance with the practice of many scholars, fifteen minutes or so could be set aside for these invocations on Thursday following the ʿIshā' prayer. This manual is also an ideal companion for one's journey to the city of the Prophet ﷺ, Madīna al-Munawwara.

One can engage in the invocation of blessings at all times and in all pure places. Being in a state of ablution, although recommended, is not required. (However, the written form of the name of Allāh should not be touched when handling the book in a state of ritual impurity.) Hence, women can read this manual even during their monthly cycles, and benefit through the invocations at a time when they are unable to perform their five daily prayers or recite the Qur'ān.

I praise Allāh for granting me the ability to work on this manual. May Allāh grant it a complete acceptance in His court, make it a source for my salvation in the Hereafter and intercession from His Most Beloved ﷺ, and a means of blessing for my family, my teachers, and all those who assisted in its production.

ABDUR-RAHMAN IBN YUSUF MANGERA
SANTA BARBARA, CALIFORNIA
Friday April 20, 2007 | Rabīʿ al-Thānī 2, 1428

محمد رسول الله

Part One

Fifty Invocations of Blessings and Peace

In the name of Allāh, Most Beneficent, Most Merciful.

Peace upon Allāh's chosen servants. Peace upon the Messengers.

Invocations of Blessings

1. O Allāh, bless Muḥammad and the family of Muḥammad, and appoint for him a blessed seat near You.

2. O Allāh, Lord of this firm call and beneficial prayer, bless Muḥammad—approve of me such that You do not disapprove of me ever after.

3. O Allāh, bless Muḥammad, Your servant and Your Messenger, and bless every Believer, man and woman, and every Muslim, man and woman.

4. O Allāh, bless Muḥammad and the family of Muḥammad, and favor Muḥammad and the family of Muḥammad, and have mercy on Muḥammad and the family of Muḥammad, just as You blessed, favored, and had mercy on Ibrāhīm and the family of Ibrāhīm. You are truly the Most Praiseworthy and Noble.

بِسْمِ اللهِ الرَّحْمٰنِ الرَّحِيْمِ

سَلَامٌ عَلٰى عِبَادِهِ الَّذِيْنَ اصْطَفٰى، سَلَامٌ عَلَى الْمُرْسَلِيْنَ

صيغ الصلاة

﴿١﴾ اَللّٰهُمَّ صَلِّ عَلٰى مُحَمَّدٍ وَّعَلٰى اٰلِ مُحَمَّدٍ وَّأَنْزِلْهُ الْمَقْعَدَ الْمُقَرَّبَ عِنْدَكَ

﴿٢﴾ اَللّٰهُمَّ رَبَّ هٰذِهِ الدَّعْوَةِ الْقَائِمَةِ وَالصَّلَاةِ النَّافِعَةِ صَلِّ عَلٰى مُحَمَّدٍ وَّارْضَ عَنِّيْ رِضًا لَّا تَسْخَطُ بَعْدَهٗ أَبَدًا

﴿٣﴾ اَللّٰهُمَّ صَلِّ عَلٰى مُحَمَّدٍ عَبْدِكَ وَرَسُوْلِكَ وَصَلِّ عَلَى الْمُؤْمِنِيْنَ وَالْمُؤْمِنَاتِ وَالْمُسْلِمِيْنَ وَالْمُسْلِمَاتِ

﴿٤﴾ اَللّٰهُمَّ صَلِّ عَلٰى مُحَمَّدٍ وَّعَلٰى اٰلِ مُحَمَّدٍ وَّبَارِكْ عَلٰى مُحَمَّدٍ وَّعَلٰى اٰلِ مُحَمَّدٍ وَّارْحَمْ مُحَمَّدًا وَّاٰلَ مُحَمَّدٍ كَمَا صَلَّيْتَ وَبَارَكْتَ وَرَحِمْتَ عَلٰى إِبْرَاهِيْمَ وَعَلٰى اٰلِ إِبْرَاهِيْمَ، إِنَّكَ حَمِيْدٌ مَّجِيْدٌ

5. O Allāh, bless Muḥammad and the family of Muḥammad as You blessed the family of Ibrāhīm, for You are truly the Most Praiseworthy and Noble. O Allāh, favor Muḥammad and the family of Muḥammad as You favored the family of Ibrāhīm, for You are truly the Most Praiseworthy and Noble.

6. O Allāh, bless Muḥammad and the family of Muḥammad as You blessed the family of Ibrāhīm, for You are truly the Most Praiseworthy and Noble. And favor Muḥammad and the family of Muḥammad as You favored the family of Ibrāhīm, for You are truly the Most Praiseworthy and Noble.

7. O Allāh, bless Muḥammad and the family of Muḥammad as You blessed Ibrāhīm, for You are truly the Most Praiseworthy and Noble. O Allāh, favor Muḥammad and the family of Muḥammad as You favored Ibrāhīm, for You are truly the Most Praiseworthy and Noble.

8. O Allāh, bless Muḥammad and the family of Muḥammad as You blessed Ibrāhīm and the family of Ibrāhīm, for You are truly the Most Praiseworthy and Noble. And favor Muḥammad and the family of Muḥammad as You favored Ibrāhīm, for You are truly the Most Praiseworthy and Noble.

﴿٥﴾ اَللّٰهُمَّ صَلِّ عَلٰى مُحَمَّدٍ وَّعَلٰى اٰلِ مُحَمَّدٍ كَمَا صَلَّيْتَ عَلٰى اٰلِ إِبْرَاهِيْمَ، إِنَّكَ حَمِيْدٌ مَّجِيْدٌ. اَللّٰهُمَّ بَارِكْ عَلٰى مُحَمَّدٍ وَّعَلٰى اٰلِ مُحَمَّدٍ كَمَا بَارَكْتَ عَلٰى اٰلِ إِبْرَاهِيْمَ، إِنَّكَ حَمِيْدٌ مَّجِيْدٌ

﴿٦﴾ اَللّٰهُمَّ صَلِّ عَلٰى مُحَمَّدٍ وَّعَلٰى اٰلِ مُحَمَّدٍ كَمَا صَلَّيْتَ عَلٰى اٰلِ إِبْرَاهِيْمَ، إِنَّكَ حَمِيْدٌ مَّجِيْدٌ، وَبَارِكْ عَلٰى مُحَمَّدٍ وَّعَلٰى اٰلِ مُحَمَّدٍ كَمَا بَارَكْتَ عَلٰى اٰلِ إِبْرَاهِيْمَ، إِنَّكَ حَمِيْدٌ مَّجِيْدٌ

﴿٧﴾ اَللّٰهُمَّ صَلِّ عَلٰى مُحَمَّدٍ وَّعَلٰى اٰلِ مُحَمَّدٍ كَمَا صَلَّيْتَ عَلٰى إِبْرَاهِيْمَ، إِنَّكَ حَمِيْدٌ مَّجِيْدٌ. اَللّٰهُمَّ بَارِكْ عَلٰى مُحَمَّدٍ وَّعَلٰى اٰلِ مُحَمَّدٍ كَمَا بَارَكْتَ عَلٰى إِبْرَاهِيْمَ، إِنَّكَ حَمِيْدٌ مَّجِيْدٌ

﴿٨﴾ اَللّٰهُمَّ صَلِّ عَلٰى مُحَمَّدٍ وَّعَلٰى اٰلِ مُحَمَّدٍ كَمَا صَلَّيْتَ عَلٰى إِبْرَاهِيْمَ، وَعَلٰى اٰلِ إِبْرَاهِيْمَ، إِنَّكَ حَمِيْدٌ مَّجِيْدٌ، وَّبَارِكْ عَلٰى مُحَمَّدٍ وَّعَلٰى اٰلِ مُحَمَّدٍ كَمَا بَارَكْتَ عَلٰى إِبْرَاهِيْمَ، إِنَّكَ حَمِيْدٌ مَّجِيْدٌ

9. O Allāh, bless Muḥammad and the family of Muḥammad as You blessed Ibrāhīm, and favor Muḥammad and the family of Muḥammad as You favored Ibrāhīm, for You are truly the Most Praiseworthy and Noble.

10. O Allāh, bless Muḥammad and the family of Muḥammad as You blessed Ibrāhīm, for You are truly the Most Praiseworthy and Noble. O Allāh, favor Muḥammad and the family of Muḥammad as You favored the family of Ibrāhīm, for You are truly the Most Praiseworthy and Noble.

11. O Allāh, bless Muḥammad and the family of Muḥammad as You blessed the family of Ibrāhīm, and favor Muḥammad and the family of Muḥammad as You favored the family of Ibrāhīm in all the worlds, for You are truly the Most Praiseworthy and Noble.

12. O Allāh, bless Muḥammad and his wives and children as You blessed the family of Ibrāhīm, and favor Muḥammad and his wives and children as You favored the family of Ibrāhīm, for You are truly the Most Praiseworthy and Noble.

﴿٩﴾ اَللّٰهُمَّ صَلِّ عَلٰى مُحَمَّدٍ وَّعَلٰى اٰلِ مُحَمَّدٍ كَمَا صَلَّيْتَ عَلٰى إِبْرَاهِيْمَ، وَبَارِكْ عَلٰى مُحَمَّدٍ وَّعَلٰى اٰلِ مُحَمَّدٍ كَمَا بَارَكْتَ عَلٰى إِبْرَاهِيْمَ، إِنَّكَ حَمِيْدٌ مَّجِيْدٌ

﴿١٠﴾ اَللّٰهُمَّ صَلِّ عَلٰى مُحَمَّدٍ وَّعَلٰى اٰلِ مُحَمَّدٍ كَمَا صَلَّيْتَ عَلٰى إِبْرَاهِيْمَ، إِنَّكَ حَمِيْدٌ مَّجِيْدٌ. اَللّٰهُمَّ بَارِكْ عَلٰى مُحَمَّدٍ وَّعَلٰى اٰلِ مُحَمَّدٍ كَمَا بَارَكْتَ عَلٰى اٰلِ إِبْرَاهِيْمَ، إِنَّكَ حَمِيْدٌ مَّجِيْدٌ

﴿١١﴾ اَللّٰهُمَّ صَلِّ عَلٰى مُحَمَّدٍ وَّعَلٰى اٰلِ مُحَمَّدٍ كَمَا صَلَّيْتَ عَلٰى اٰلِ إِبْرَاهِيْمَ، وَبَارِكْ عَلٰى مُحَمَّدٍ وَّعَلٰى اٰلِ مُحَمَّدٍ كَمَا بَارَكْتَ عَلٰى اٰلِ إِبْرَاهِيْمَ فِي الْعَالَمِيْنَ، إِنَّكَ حَمِيْدٌ مَّجِيْدٌ

﴿١٢﴾ اَللّٰهُمَّ صَلِّ عَلٰى مُحَمَّدٍ وَّأَزْوَاجِهٖ وَذُرِّيَّتِهٖ كَمَا صَلَّيْتَ عَلٰى اٰلِ إِبْرَاهِيْمَ، وَبَارِكْ عَلٰى مُحَمَّدٍ وَّأَزْوَاجِهٖ وَذُرِّيَّتِهٖ كَمَا بَارَكْتَ عَلٰى اٰلِ إِبْرَاهِيْمَ، إِنَّكَ حَمِيْدٌ مَّجِيْدٌ

13. O Allāh, bless Muḥammad and his wives and children as You blessed the family of Ibrāhīm, and favor Muḥammad and his wives and children as You favored the family of Ibrāhīm, for You are truly the Most Praiseworthy and Noble.

14. O Allāh, bless the Prophet Muḥammad, and his wives, the Mothers of the Believers, and his children, and the people of his house, as You blessed Ibrāhīm, for You are truly the Most Praiseworthy and Noble.

15. O Allāh, bless Muḥammad and the family of Muḥammad as You blessed Ibrāhīm and the family of Ibrāhīm, and favor Muḥammad and the family of Muḥammad as You favored Ibrāhīm, and have mercy on Muḥammad and the family of Muḥammad as You had mercy on Ibrāhīm and the family of Ibrāhīm.

16. O Allāh, bless Muḥammad and the family of Muḥammad as You blessed Ibrāhīm and the family of Ibrāhīm, for You are truly the Most Praiseworthy and Noble. O Allāh, favor Muḥammad and the family of Muḥammad as You favored Ibrāhīm and the family of Ibrāhīm, for You are truly the Most Praiseworthy

﴿١٣﴾ اَللّٰهُمَّ صَلِّ عَلٰى مُحَمَّدٍ وَّعَلٰى أَزْوَاجِهٖ وَذُرِّيَّتِهٖ كَمَا صَلَّيْتَ عَلٰى اٰلِ إِبْرَاهِيْمَ، وَبَارِكْ عَلٰى مُحَمَّدٍ وَّعَلٰى أَزْوَاجِهٖ وَذُرِّيَّتِهٖ كَمَا بَارَكْتَ عَلٰى اٰلِ إِبْرَاهِيْمَ، إِنَّكَ حَمِيْدٌ مَّجِيْدٌ

﴿١٤﴾ اَللّٰهُمَّ صَلِّ عَلٰى مُحَمَّدِنِ النَّبِيِّ وَأَزْوَاجِهٖ أُمَّهَاتِ الْمُؤْمِنِيْنَ وَذُرِّيَّتِهٖ وَأَهْلِ بَيْتِهٖ كَمَا صَلَّيْتَ عَلٰى إِبْرَاهِيْمَ، إِنَّكَ حَمِيْدٌ مَّجِيْدٌ

﴿١٥﴾ اَللّٰهُمَّ صَلِّ عَلٰى مُحَمَّدٍ وَّعَلٰى اٰلِ مُحَمَّدٍ كَمَا صَلَّيْتَ عَلٰى إِبْرَاهِيْمَ وَعَلٰى اٰلِ إِبْرَاهِيْمَ، وَبَارِكْ عَلٰى مُحَمَّدٍ وَّعَلٰى اٰلِ مُحَمَّدٍ كَمَا بَارَكْتَ عَلٰى إِبْرَاهِيْمَ، وَتَرَحَّمْ عَلٰى مُحَمَّدٍ وَّعَلٰى اٰلِ مُحَمَّدٍ كَمَا تَرَحَّمْتَ عَلٰى إِبْرَاهِيْمَ وَعَلٰى اٰلِ إِبْرَاهِيْمَ

﴿١٦﴾ اَللّٰهُمَّ صَلِّ عَلٰى مُحَمَّدٍ وَّعَلٰى اٰلِ مُحَمَّدٍ كَمَا صَلَّيْتَ عَلٰى إِبْرَاهِيْمَ وَعَلٰى اٰلِ إِبْرَاهِيْمَ، إِنَّكَ حَمِيْدٌ مَّجِيْدٌ. اَللّٰهُمَّ بَارِكْ عَلٰى مُحَمَّدٍ وَّعَلٰى اٰلِ مُحَمَّدٍ كَمَا بَارَكْتَ عَلٰى إِبْرَاهِيْمَ وَعَلٰى اٰلِ إِبْرَاهِيْمَ، إِنَّكَ حَمِيْدٌ مَّجِيْدٌ.

and Noble. O Allāh, have mercy on Muḥammad and the family of Muḥammad as You had mercy on Ibrāhīm and the family of Ibrāhīm, for You are truly the Most Praiseworthy and Noble. O Allāh, love Muḥammad and the family of Muḥammad as You loved Ibrāhīm and the family of Ibrāhīm, for You are truly the Most Praiseworthy and Noble. O Allāh, bestow peace on Muḥammad and the family of Muḥammad as You bestowed peace on Ibrāhīm and the family of Ibrāhīm, for You are truly the Most Praiseworthy and Noble.

17. O Allāh, bless Muḥammad and the family of Muḥammad, and favor and bestow peace on Muḥammad and on the family of Muḥammad, and have mercy on Muḥammad and the family of Muḥammad, as You blessed, favored, and had mercy on Ibrāhīm and the family of Ibrāhīm in the worlds, for You are truly the Most Praiseworthy and Noble.

18. O Allāh, bless Muḥammad and the family of Muḥammad as You blessed Ibrāhīm and the family of Ibrāhīm, for You are truly the Most Praiseworthy and Noble. O Allāh, favor Muḥammad and the family of Muḥammad as You favored Ibrāhīm and the family of Ibrāhīm, for You are truly the Most Praiseworthy and Noble.

اَللّٰهُمَّ تَرَحَّمْ عَلٰى مُحَمَّدٍ وَّعَلٰى اٰلِ مُحَمَّدٍ كَمَا تَرَحَّمْتَ عَلٰى إِبْرَاهِيْمَ وَعَلٰى اٰلِ إِبْرَاهِيْمَ، إِنَّكَ حَمِيْدٌ مَّجِيْدٌ. اَللّٰهُمَّ تَحَنَّنْ عَلٰى مُحَمَّدٍ وَّعَلٰى اٰلِ مُحَمَّدٍ كَمَا تَحَنَّنْتَ عَلٰى إِبْرَاهِيْمَ وَعَلٰى اٰلِ إِبْرَاهِيْمَ، إِنَّكَ حَمِيْدٌ مَّجِيْدٌ. اَللّٰهُمَّ سَلِّمْ عَلٰى مُحَمَّدٍ وَّعَلٰى اٰلِ مُحَمَّدٍ كَمَا سَلَّمْتَ عَلٰى إِبْرَاهِيْمَ وَعَلٰى اٰلِ إِبْرَاهِيْمَ، إِنَّكَ حَمِيْدٌ مَّجِيْدٌ

﴿١٧﴾ اَللّٰهُمَّ صَلِّ عَلٰى مُحَمَّدٍ وَّعَلٰى اٰلِ مُحَمَّدٍ، وَّبَارِكْ وَسَلِّمْ عَلٰى مُحَمَّدٍ وَّعَلٰى اٰلِ مُحَمَّدٍ، وَّارْحَمْ مُحَمَّدًا وَّاٰلَ مُحَمَّدٍ كَمَا صَلَّيْتَ وَبَارَكْتَ وَتَرَحَّمْتَ عَلٰى إِبْرَاهِيْمَ وعَلٰى اٰلِ إِبْرَاهِيْمَ فِي الْعَالَمِيْنَ، إِنَّكَ حَمِيْدٌ مَّجِيْدٌ

﴿١٨﴾ اَللّٰهُمَّ صَلِّ عَلٰى مُحَمَّدٍ وَّعَلٰى اٰلِ مُحَمَّدٍ كَمَا صَلَّيْتَ عَلٰى إِبْرَاهِيْمَ وَعَلٰى اٰلِ إِبْرَاهِيْمَ، إِنَّكَ حَمِيْدٌ مَّجِيْدٌ. اَللّٰهُمَّ بَارِكْ عَلٰى مُحَمَّدٍ وَّعَلٰى اٰلِ مُحَمَّدٍ كَمَا بَارَكْتَ عَلٰى إِبْرَاهِيْمَ وَعَلٰى اٰلِ إِبْرَاهِيْمَ، إِنَّكَ حَمِيْدٌ مَّجِيْدٌ

19. O Allāh, bless Your servant and Messenger, Muḥammad, as You blessed the family of Ibrāhīm, and favor Muḥammad and the family of Muḥammad as You favored the family of Ibrāhīm.

20. O Allāh, bless the Unlettered Prophet Muḥammad and the family of Muḥammad as You blessed Ibrāhīm, and favor the Unlettered Prophet Muḥammad as You favored Ibrāhīm, for You are truly the Most Praiseworthy and Noble.

21. O Allāh, bless Your servant and Messenger, the Unlettered Prophet Muḥammad, and the family of Muḥammad. O Allāh, bless Muḥammad and the family of Muḥammad, with blessings that are the source of Your pleasure [with him], a reward for him, and a fulfillment of his rights. Grant him a seat near You, an excellent and exalted degree, and the worthy station You have promised him. Grant him a fitting reward on our behalf, and grant him the best return You have granted any prophet on behalf of his people or any messenger on behalf of his nation, and bless all his brethren among the prophets and righteous, O Most Merciful of the merciful.

﴿١٩﴾ اَللّٰهُمَّ صَلِّ عَلٰى مُحَمَّدٍ عَبْدِكَ وَرَسُوْلِكَ كَمَا صَلَّيْتَ عَلٰى اٰلِ إِبْرَاهِيْمَ، وَبَارِكْ عَلٰى مُحَمَّدٍ وَّعَلٰى اٰلِ مُحَمَّدٍ كَمَا بَارَكْتَ عَلٰى اٰلِ إِبْرَاهِيْمَ

﴿٢٠﴾ اَللّٰهُمَّ صَلِّ عَلٰى مُحَمَّدِنِ النَّبِيِّ الْأُمِّيِّ وَعَلٰى اٰلِ مُحَمَّدٍ كَمَا صَلَّيْتَ عَلٰى إِبْرَاهِيْمَ، وَبَارِكْ عَلٰى مُحَمَّدِنِ النَّبِيِّ الْأُمِّيِّ كَمَا بَارَكْتَ عَلٰى إِبْرَاهِيْمَ، إِنَّكَ حَمِيْدٌ مَّجِيْدٌ

﴿٢١﴾ اَللّٰهُمَّ صَلِّ عَلٰى مُحَمَّدٍ عَبْدِكَ وَرَسُوْلِكَ النَّبِيِّ الْأُمِّيِّ وَعَلٰى اٰلِ مُحَمَّدٍ. اَللّٰهُمَّ صَلِّ عَلٰى مُحَمَّدٍ وَّعَلٰى اٰلِ مُحَمَّدٍ صَلَاةً تَكُوْنُ لَكَ رِضًى وَّلَهٗ جَزَاءً وَّلِحَقِّهٖ أَدَاءً، وَّأَعْطِهِ الْوَسِيْلَةَ وَالْفَضِيْلَةَ وَالْمَقَامَ الْمَحْمُوْدَ الَّذِيْ وَعَدتَّهٗ، وَاجْزِهٖ عَنَّا مَا هُوَ أَهْلُهٗ، وَاجْزِهٖ أَفْضَلَ مَا جَازَيْتَ نَبِيًّا عَنْ قَوْمِهٖ وَرَسُوْلًا عَنْ أُمَّتِهٖ، وَصَلِّ عَلٰى جَمِيْعِ إِخْوَانِهٖ مِنَ النَّبِيِّيْنَ وَالصَّالِحِيْنَ، يَا أَرْحَمَ الرَّاحِمِيْنَ

22. O Allāh, bless the Unlettered Prophet Muḥammad and the family of Muḥammad, as You blessed Ibrāhīm and the family of Ibrāhīm, and favor the Unlettered Prophet Muḥammad and the family of Muḥammad, as You favored Ibrāhīm and the family of Ibrāhīm, for You are truly the Most Praiseworthy and Noble.

23. O Allāh, bless Muḥammad and the people of his house as You blessed Ibrāhīm, for You are truly the Most Praiseworthy and Noble. O Allāh, bless us with them. O Allāh, favor Muḥammad and the people of his house as You favored Ibrāhīm, for You are truly the Most Praiseworthy and Noble. O Allāh, favor us with them. The blessings of Allāh and the blessings of the Believers be upon the Unlettered Prophet, Muḥammad.

24. O Allāh, shower Your blessings, mercy, and favors on Muḥammad and the family of Muḥammad, as You have showered them on the family of Ibrāhīm, for You are truly the Most Praiseworthy and Noble. And favor Muḥammad and the family of Muḥammad, as You favored Ibrāhīm and the family of Ibrāhīm, for You are truly the Most Praiseworthy and Noble.

25. And may Allāh send His mercy on the Unlettered Prophet.

﴿٢٢﴾ اَللّٰهُمَّ صَلِّ عَلٰى مُحَمَّدِنِ النَّبِيِّ الْأُمِّيِّ وَعَلٰى أٰلِ مُحَمَّدٍ كَمَا صَلَّيْتَ عَلٰى إِبْرَاهِيْمَ وَعَلٰى أٰلِ إِبْرَاهِيْمَ، وَبَارِكْ عَلٰى مُحَمَّدِنِ النَّبِيِّ الْأُمِّيِّ وَعَلٰى أٰلِ مُحَمَّدٍ كَمَا بَارَكْتَ عَلٰى إِبْرَاهِيْمَ وَعَلٰى أٰلِ إِبْرَاهِيْمَ، إِنَّكَ حَمِيْدٌ مَّجِيْدٌ

﴿٢٣﴾ اَللّٰهُمَّ صَلِّ عَلٰى مُحَمَّدٍ وَّعَلٰى أَهْلِ بَيْتِهٖ كَمَا صَلَّيْتَ عَلٰى إِبْرَاهِيْمَ، إِنَّكَ حَمِيْدٌ مَّجِيْدٌ. اَللّٰهُمَّ صَلِّ عَلَيْنَا مَعَهُمْ. اَللّٰهُمَّ بَارِكْ عَلٰى مُحَمَّدٍ وَّعَلٰى أَهْلِ بَيْتِهٖ كَمَا بَارَكْتَ عَلٰى إِبْرَاهِيْمَ، إِنَّكَ حَمِيْدٌ مَّجِيْدٌ. اَللّٰهُمَّ بَارِكْ عَلَيْنَا مَعَهُمْ. صَلَوَاتُ اللهِ وَصَلَوَاتُ الْمُؤْمِنِيْنَ عَلٰى مُحَمَّدِنِ النَّبِيِّ الْأُمِّيِّ

﴿٢٤﴾ اَللّٰهُمَّ اجْعَلْ صَلَوَاتِكَ وَرَحْمَتَكَ وَبَرَكَاتِكَ عَلٰى مُحَمَّدٍ وَّعَلٰى أٰلِ مُحَمَّدٍ كَمَا جَعَلْتَهَا عَلٰى أٰلِ إِبْرَاهِيْمَ، إِنَّكَ حَمِيْدٌ مَّجِيْدٌ، وَبَارِكْ عَلٰى مُحَمَّدٍ وَّعَلٰى أٰلِ مُحَمَّدٍ كَمَا بَارَكْتَ عَلٰى إِبْرَاهِيْمَ وَعَلٰى أٰلِ إِبْرَاهِيْمَ، إِنَّكَ حَمِيْدٌ مَّجِيْدٌ

﴿٢٥﴾ وَصَلَّى اللهُ عَلٰى النَّبِيِّ الْأُمِّيِّ

Invocations of Peace

26. Salutations to Allāh, and blessings and pure worship. Peace be upon you, O Prophet, and the mercy of Allāh and His favors. Peace be upon us and the righteous servants of Allāh. I testify that there is no god but Allāh, and I testify that Muḥammad is His servant and Messenger.

27. Salutations, pure worship, and blessings are for Allāh. Peace be upon you, O Prophet, and the mercy of Allāh and His favors. Peace be upon us and the righteous servants of Allāh. I testify that there is no god but Allāh, and I testify that Muḥammad is His servant and Messenger.

28. Salutations to Allāh, and pure worship and blessings are for Allāh. Peace be upon you, O Prophet, and the mercy of Allāh and His favors. Peace be upon us and the righteous servants of Allāh. I testify that there is no god but Allāh alone who has no partner, and I testify that Muḥammad is His servant and Messenger.

29. Salutations, blessings, and pure worship are for Allāh.

صيغ السلام

﴿٢٦﴾ اَلتَّحِيَّاتُ لِلّٰهِ وَالصَّلَوَاتُ وَالطَّيِّبَاتُ، السَّلَامُ عَلَيْكَ أَيُّهَا النَّبِيُّ وَرَحْمَةُ اللهِ وَبَرَكَاتُهُ، السَّلَامُ عَلَيْنَا وَعَلٰى عِبَادِ اللهِ الصَّالِحِيْنَ. أَشْهَدُ أَن لَّا إِلٰهَ إِلَّا اللهُ وَأَشْهَدُ أَنَّ مُحَمَّدًا عَبْدُهُ وَرَسُوْلُهُ

﴿٢٧﴾ اَلتَّحِيَّاتُ الطَّيِّبَاتُ الصَّلَوَاتُ لِلّٰهِ، السَّلَامُ عَلَيْكَ أَيُّهَا النَّبِيُّ وَرَحْمَةُ اللهِ وَبَرَكَاتُهُ، السَّلَامُ عَلَيْنَا وَعَلٰى عِبَادِ اللهِ الصَّالِحِيْنَ. أَشْهَدُ أَن لَّا إِلٰهَ إِلَّا اللهُ وَأَشْهَدُ أَنَّ مُحَمَّدًا عَبْدُهُ وَرَسُوْلُهُ

﴿٢٨﴾ اَلتَّحِيَّاتُ لِلّٰهِ الطَّيِّبَاتُ الصَّلَوَاتُ لِلّٰهِ، السَّلَامُ عَلَيْكَ أَيُّهَا النَّبِيُّ وَرَحْمَةُ اللهِ وَبَرَكَاتُهُ، السَّلَامُ عَلَيْنَا وَعَلٰى عِبَادِ اللهِ الصَّالِحِيْنَ. أَشْهَدُ أَن لَّا إِلٰهَ إِلَّا اللهُ وَحْدَهُ لَا شَرِيْكَ لَهُ وَأَشْهَدُ أَنَّ مُحَمَّدًا عَبْدُهُ وَرَسُوْلُهُ

﴿٢٩﴾ اَلتَّحِيَّاتُ الْمُبَارَكَاتُ الصَّلَوَاتُ الطَّيِّبَاتُ لِلّٰهِ، سَلَامٌ عَلَيْكَ

Peace be upon you, O Prophet, and the mercy of Allāh and His favors. Peace be upon us and the righteous servants of Allāh. I testify that there is no god but Allāh, and I testify that Muḥammad is His servant and Messenger.

30. In the Name of Allāh, and by Allāh. Salutations to Allāh, blessings and pure worship are for Him. Peace be upon you, O Prophet, and the mercy of Allāh and His favors. Peace be upon us and the righteous servants of Allāh. I testify that there is no god but Allāh, and I testify that Muḥammad is His servant and Messenger. I ask Allāh for the Garden and seek Allāh's refuge from the Fire.

31. Salutations to Allāh, the wholesome is for Allāh, and pure worship and blessings are for Allāh. Peace be upon you, O Prophet, and the mercy of Allāh and His favors. Peace be upon us and the righteous servants of Allāh. I testify that there is no god but Allāh, and I testify that Muḥammad is His servant and Messenger.

32. In the Name of Allāh, and by Allāh the best of names. Salutations, pure worship, and blessings are for Allāh. I testify that there is no god but Allāh alone who has no partner, and I

أَيُّهَا النَّبِيُّ وَرَحْمَةُ اللهِ وَبَرَكَاتُهُ، سَلَامٌ عَلَيْنَا وَعَلٰى عِبَادِ اللهِ الصَّالِحِيْنَ.
أَشْهَدُ أَن لَّا إِلٰهَ إِلَّا اللهُ وَأَشْهَدُ أَنَّ مُحَمَّدًا عَبْدُهُ وَرَسُوْلُهُ

﴿٣٠﴾ بِسْمِ اللهِ وَبِاللهِ، التَّحِيَّاتُ لِلّٰهِ وَالصَّلَوَاتُ وَالطَّيِّبَاتُ، السَّلَامُ عَلَيْكَ أَيُّهَا النَّبِيُّ وَرَحْمَةُ اللهِ وَبَرَكَاتُهُ، السَّلَامُ عَلَيْنَا وَعَلٰى عِبَادِ اللهِ الصَّالِحِيْنَ. أَشْهَدُ أَن لَّا إِلٰهَ إِلَّا اللهُ وَأَشْهَدُ أَنَّ مُحَمَّدًا عَبْدُهُ وَرَسُوْلُهُ. أَسأَلُ اللهَ الْجَنَّةَ وَأَعُوْذُ بِاللهِ مِنَ النَّارِ

﴿٣١﴾ اَلتَّحِيَّاتُ لِلّٰهِ الزَّاكِيَاتُ لِلّٰهِ الطَّيِّبَاتُ الصَّلَوَاتُ لِلّٰهِ، السَّلَامُ عَلَيْكَ أَيُّهَا النَّبِيُّ وَرَحْمَةُ اللهِ وَبَرَكَاتُهُ، السَّلَامُ عَلَيْنَا وَعَلٰى عِبَادِ اللهِ الصَّالِحِيْنَ. أَشْهَدُ أَن لَّا إِلٰهَ إِلَّا اللهُ وَأَشْهَدُ أَنَّ مُحَمَّدًا عَبْدُهُ وَرَسُوْلُهُ

﴿٣٢﴾ بِسْمِ اللهِ وَبِاللهِ خَيْرِ الْأَسْمَاءِ، التَّحِيَّاتُ الطَّيِّبَاتُ الصَّلَوَاتُ لِلّٰهِ.
أَشْهَدُ أَن لَّا إِلٰهَ إِلَّا اللهُ وَحْدَهُ لَا شَرِيْكَ لَهُ وَأَشْهَدُ أَنَّ مُحَمَّدًا عَبْدُهُ

testify that Muḥammad is His servant and Messenger whom He sent with the truth as a giver of glad tidings and a warner, and that the Final Hour is without doubt to come. Peace be upon you, O Prophet, and the mercy of Allāh and His favors. Peace be upon us and the righteous servants of Allāh. O Allāh, forgive me and guide me aright.

33. Salutations, pure worship, blessings, and the dominion are for Allāh. Peace be upon you, O Prophet, and the mercy of Allāh and His favors.

34. In the Name of Allāh. Salutations to Allāh, blessings are for Allāh, and the wholesome is for Allāh. Peace be upon the Prophet, and the mercy of Allāh and His favors. Peace be upon us and the righteous servants of Allāh. I have testified that there is no god but Allāh, and I have testified that Muḥammad is Allāh's Messenger.

35. Salutations, pure worship, blessings, and the wholesome are for Allāh. I testify that there is no god but Allāh alone who has no partner, and that Muḥammad is His servant and Messenger. Peace be upon you, O Prophet, and the mercy of Allāh and His favors. Peace be upon us and the righteous servants of Allāh.

وَرَسُوْلُهُ، أَرْسَلَهُ بِالْحَقِّ بَشِيْرًا وَّنَذِيرًا وَّأَنَّ السَّاعَةَ أٰتِيَةٌ لَّا رَيْبَ فِيْهَا. السَّلَامُ عَلَيْكَ أَيُّهَا النَّبِيُّ وَرَحْمَةُ اللهِ وَبَرَكَاتُهُ، السَّلَامُ عَلَيْنَا وَعَلٰى عِبَادِ اللهِ الصَّالِحِيْنَ. اللّٰهُمَّ اغْفِرْ لِيْ وَاهْدِنِيْ

﴿٣٣﴾ اَلتَّحِيَّاتُ الطَّيِّبَاتُ وَالصَّلَوَاتُ وَالْمُلْكُ لِلّٰهِ، السَّلَامُ عَلَيْكَ أَيُّهَا النَّبِيُّ وَرَحْمَةُ اللهِ وَبَرَكَاتُهُ

﴿٣٤﴾ بِسْمِ اللهِ، التَّحِيَّاتُ لِلّٰهِ الصَّلَوَاتُ لِلّٰهِ الزَّاكِيَاتُ لِلّٰهِ، السَّلَامُ عَلَى النَّبِيِّ وَرَحْمَةُ اللهِ وَبَرَكَاتُهُ، السَّلَامُ عَلَيْنَا وَعَلٰى عِبَادِ اللهِ الصَّالِحِيْنَ. شَهِدتُّ أَن لَّا إِلٰهَ إِلَّا اللهُ شَهِدتُّ أَنَّ مُحَمَّدًا رَّسُوْلُ اللهِ

﴿٣٥﴾ اَلتَّحِيَّاتُ الطَّيِّبَاتُ الصَّلَوَاتُ الزَّاكِيَاتُ لِلّٰهِ. أَشْهَدُ أَن لَّا إِلٰهَ إِلَّا اللهُ وَحْدَهُ لَا شَرِيْكَ لَهُ وَأَنَّ مُحَمَّدًا عَبْدُهُ وَرَسُوْلُهُ. السَّلَامُ عَلَيْكَ أَيُّهَا النَّبِيُّ وَرَحْمَةُ اللهِ وَبَرَكَاتُهُ، السَّلَامُ عَلَيْنَا وَعَلٰى عِبَادِ اللهِ الصَّالِحِيْنَ

36. Salutations, pure worship, blessings, and the wholesome are for Allāh. I testify that there is no god but Allāh, and I testify that Muḥammad is Allāh's servant and Messenger. Peace be upon you, O Prophet, and the mercy of Allāh and His favors. Peace be upon us and the righteous servants of Allāh.

37. Salutations and blessings are for Allāh. Peace be upon you, O Prophet, and the mercy of Allāh and His favors. Peace be upon us and the righteous servants of Allāh.

38. Salutations to Allāh, and blessings and pure worship. Peace be upon you, O Prophet, and the mercy of Allāh. Peace be upon us and the righteous servants of Allāh. I testify that there is no god but Allāh, and I testify that Muḥammad is His servant and Messenger.

39. Salutations, blessings, and pure worship are for Allāh. Peace be upon you, O Prophet, and the mercy of Allāh and His favors. Peace be upon us and the righteous servants of Allāh. I testify that there is no god but Allāh, and I testify that Muḥammad is Allāh's Messenger.

40. In the name of Allāh, and peace upon the Messenger of Allāh.

﴿٣٦﴾ اَلتَّحِيَّاتُ الطَّيِّبَاتُ الصَّلَوَاتُ الزَّاكِيَاتُ لِلّٰهِ. أَشْهَدُ أَن لَّا إِلٰهَ إِلَّا اللهُ وَأَشْهَدُ أَنَّ مُحَمَّدًا عَبْدُ اللهِ وَرَسُوْلُهٗ. السَّلَامُ عَلَيْكَ أَيُّهَا النَّبِيُّ وَرَحْمَةُ اللهِ وَبَرَكَاتُهٗ، السَّلَامُ عَلَيْنَا وَعَلٰى عِبَادِ اللهِ الصَّالِحِيْنَ

﴿٣٧﴾ اَلتَّحِيَّاتُ الصَّلَوَاتُ لِلّٰهِ السَّلَامُ عَلَيْكَ أَيُّهَا النَّبِيُّ وَرَحْمَةُ اللهِ وَبَرَكَاتُهٗ، السَّلَامُ عَلَيْنَا وَعَلٰى عِبَادِ اللهِ الصَّالِحِيْنَ

﴿٣٨﴾ اَلتَّحِيَّاتُ لِلّٰهِ الصَّلَوَاتُ الطَّيِّبَاتُ، السَّلَامُ عَلَيْكَ أَيُّهَا النَّبِيُّ وَرَحْمَةُ اللهِ، السَّلَامُ عَلَيْنَا وَعَلٰى عِبَادِ اللهِ الصَّالِحِيْنَ. أَشْهَدُ أَن لَّا إِلٰهَ إِلَّا اللهُ وَأَشْهَدُ أَنَّ مُحَمَّدًا عَبْدُهٗ وَرَسُوْلُهٗ

﴿٣٩﴾ اَلتَّحِيَّاتُ الْمُبَارَكَاتُ الصَّلَوَاتُ الطَّيِّبَاتُ لِلّٰهِ، السَّلَامُ عَلَيْكَ أَيُّهَا النَّبِيُّ وَرَحْمَةُ اللهِ وَبَرَكَاتُهٗ، السَّلَامُ عَلَيْنَا وَعَلٰى عِبَادِ اللهِ الصَّالِحِيْنَ. أَشْهَدُ أَن لَّا إِلٰهَ إِلَّا اللهُ وَأَشْهَدُ أَنَّ مُحَمَّدًا رَّسُوْلُ اللهِ

﴿٤٠﴾ بِسْمِ اللهِ، وَالسَّلَامُ عَلٰى رَسُوْلِ اللهِ

Additional Invocations

41. O Allāh, bless the spirit of Muḥammad among the spirits, bless the body of Muḥammad among the bodies, and bless the grave of Muḥammad among the graves.

42. O Allāh, bless Muḥammad until none of Your blessings remain, favor Muḥammad until none of Your favors remain, and bestow peace upon Muḥammad until none of Your peace remains.

43. O Allāh, bless Muḥammad [with blessings] filling this world and the hereafter, favor Muḥammad [with favors] filling this world and the hereafter, have mercy upon Muḥammad [with mercy] filling this world and the hereafter, and bestow peace upon Muḥammad [with peace] filling this world and the hereafter.

44. O Allāh, bless our liegelord Muḥammad whose light preceded creation and whose appearance was a mercy for the worlds, [blessings] equal to the number of Your created beings who have passed and who remain, who are fortunate and who

باب آخر من الصلاة والسلام

﴿٤١﴾ اَللّٰهُمَّ صَلِّ عَلٰى رُوْحِ مُحَمَّدٍ فِي الْأَرْوَاحِ، وَصَلِّ عَلٰى جَسَدِ مُحَمَّدٍ فِي الْأَجْسَادِ، وَصَلِّ عَلٰى قَبْرِ مُحَمَّدٍ فِي الْقُبُوْرِ

﴿٤٢﴾ اَللّٰهُمَّ صَلِّ عَلٰى مُحَمَّدٍ حَتّٰى لَا يَبْقٰى مِنْ صَلَوَاتِكَ شَيْءٌ، وَّبَارِكْ عَلٰى مُحَمَّدٍ حَتّٰى لَا يَبْقٰى مِنْ بَرَكَاتِكَ شَيْءٌ، وَّسَلِّمْ عَلٰى مُحَمَّدٍ حَتّٰى لَا يَبْقٰى مِنْ سَلَامِكَ شَيْءٌ

﴿٤٣﴾ اَللّٰهُمَّ صَلِّ عَلٰى مُحَمَّدٍ مِّلْءَ الدُّنْيَا وَمِلْءَ الْأٰخِرَةِ، وَبَارِكْ عَلٰى مُحَمَّدٍ مِّلْءَ الدُّنْيَا وَمِلْءَ الْأٰخِرَةِ، وَّارْحَمْ مُحَمَّدً مِّلْءَ الدُّنْيَا وَمِلْءَ الْأٰخِرَةِ، وَسَلِّمْ عَلٰى مُحَمَّدٍ مِّلْءَ الدُّنْيَا وَمِلْءَ الْأٰخِرَةِ

﴿٤٤﴾ اَللّٰهُمَّ صَلِّ عَلٰى سَيِّدِنَا مُحَمَّدِنِ السَّابِقِ لِلْخَلْقِ نُوْرُهٗ، وَالرَّحْمَةِ لِلْعَالَمِيْنَ ظُهُوْرُهٗ، عَدَدَ مَنْ مَّضٰى مِنْ خَلْقِكَ وَمَنْ بَقِيَ، وَمَنْ سَعِدَ

are wretched, blessings that use up all numbers and encompass all borders, blessings with no limits nor bounds, no term nor end, blessings that last as long as You last, and the like of it upon his family and Companions. And for this may Allāh be praised.

45. O Allāh, accept Muḥammad's great intercession, raise his high rank, and grant him his requests in the hereafter and the former, just as You have given [the same to] Ibrāhīm and Mūsā.

46. O Allāh, bless Muḥammad equal to the number of those who bless him, bless Muḥammad equal to the number of those who do not bless him, bless Muḥammad as You command he be blessed, bless Muḥammad as he loves to be blessed, and bless Muḥammad as it befits him to be blessed.

47. O Allāh, I ask you, O Allāh, O Gracious, O Merciful, O Refuge of those who seek refuge, O Shelter of the fearful, O Stay of those who have no stay, O Support of those who have no support, O Resource for those who have no resource, O Sanctuary of the weak, Treasure of the needy,

مِنْهُمْ وَمَنْ شَقِيَ، صَلَاةً تَسْتَغْرِقُ الْعَدَّ وَتُحِيْطُ بِالْحَدِّ، صَلَاةً لَّا غَايَةَ لَهَا وَلَا انْتِهَاءَ، وَلَا أَمَدَ لَهَا وَلَا انْقِضَاءَ، صَلَاةً دَائِمَةً بِدَوَامِكَ، وَعَلٰى أٰلِهٖ وَصَحْبِهٖ كَذٰلِكَ. وَالْحَمْدُ لِلّٰهِ عَلٰى ذٰالِكَ

﴿٤٥﴾ اَللّٰهُمَّ تَقَبَّلْ شَفَاعَةَ مُحَمَّدِنِ الْكُبْرٰى، وَارْفَعْ دَرَجَتَهُ الْعُلْيَا، وَأَعْطِهٖ سُؤْلَهٗ فِي الْأٰخِرَةِ وَالْأُوْلٰى، كَمَا أٰتَيْتَ إِبْرَاهِيْمَ وَمُوْسٰى

﴿٤٦﴾ اَللّٰهُمَّ صَلِّ عَلٰى مُحَمَّدٍ عَدَدَ مَنْ صَلّٰى عَلَيْهِ، وَصَلِّ عَلٰى مُحَمَّدٍ بِعَدَدِ مَن لَّمْ يُصَلِّ عَلَيْهِ، وَصَلِّ عَلٰى مُحَمَّدٍ كَمَا أَمَرْتَ أَن يُّصَلّٰى عَلَيْهِ، وَصَلِّ عَلٰى مُحَمَّدٍ كَمَا يُحِبُّ أَن يُّصَلّٰى عَلَيْهِ، وَصَلِّ عَلٰى مُحَمَّدٍ كَمَا تَنْبَغِي الصَّلَاةُ عَلَيْهِ

﴿٤٧﴾ اَللّٰهُمَّ إِنِّيْ أَسْأَلُكَ يَا اَللّٰهُ، يَا رَحْمٰنُ، يَا رَحِيْمُ، يَا جَارَ الْمُسْتَجِيْرِيْنَ، يَا أَمَانَ الْخَائِفِيْنَ، يَا عِمَادَ مَن لَّا عِمَادَ لَهٗ، يَا سَنَدَ مَن لَّا سَنَدَ لَهٗ، يَا ذُخْرَ مَن لَّا ذُخْرَ لَهٗ، يَا حِرْزَ الضُّعَفَاءِ، يَا كَنْزَ الْفُقَرَاءِ، يَا

Greatest source of hope, Saviour of the doomed, Rescuer of the drowned, Beneficent, Gracious, Benefactor, Bountiful, Almighty, Omnipotent, and Effulgent—it is You to whom the darkness of the night, the brightness of the day, the rays of the sun, the trembling of the trees, the humming of water, and the light of the moon prostrate. O Allāh, You are Allāh, You have no partner. I ask that Your blessings be on our liegelord Muḥammad, Your servant and Messenger, and on the family of Muḥammad.

48. O Allāh, bless Muḥammad, the family of Muḥammad, his Companions, his children, his household, his progeny, his beloved, his followers, his supporters, and all of us with them, O Most Merciful of the merciful.

49. O Allāh, bless Muḥammad with blessings by which You save us from all dangers and misfortunes, by which You fulfil for us all our needs, by which You purify us from all our evil, by which You elevate us to a high rank by You, by which You cause us to reach the furthest limits of all good, in this world and after death. You truly have power over all things.

عَظِيْمَ الرَّجَاءِ، يَا مُنْقِذَ الْهَلْكٰى، يَا مُنْجِي الْغَرْقٰى، يَا مُحْسِنُ، يَا مُجْمِلُ، يَا مُنْعِمُ، يَا مُفْضِلُ، يَا عَزِيْزُ، يَا جَبَّارُ، يَا مُنِيْرُ، أَنْتَ الَّذِيْ سَجَدَ لَكَ سَوَادُ اللَّيْلِ، وَضَوْءُ النَّهَارِ، وَشُعَاءُ الشَّمْسِ، وَخَفِيْقُ الشَّجَرِ، وَدَوِيُّ الْمَاءِ، وَنُوْرُ الْقَمَرِ، يَا اَللهُ، أَنْتَ اللهُ، لَا شَرِيْكَ لَكَ، أَسْأَلُكَ أَنْ تُصَلِّ عَلٰى مُحَمَّدٍ عَبْدِكَ وَرَسُوْلِكَ وَعَلٰى اٰلِ مُحَمَّدٍ

﴿٤٨﴾ اَللّٰهُمَّ صَلِّ عَلٰى مُحَمَّدٍ وَّعَلٰى اٰلِ مُحَمَّدٍ وَّأَصْحَابِهٖ وَأَوْلَادِهٖ وَأَهْلِ بَيْتِهٖ وَذُرِّيَّتِهٖ وَمُحِبِّيْهِ وَأَتْبَاعِهٖ وَأَشْيَاعِهٖ، وَعَلَيْنَا مَعَهُمْ أَجْمَعِيْنَ، يَا أَرْحَمَ الرَّاحِمِيْنَ

﴿٤٩﴾ اَللّٰهُمَّ صَلِّ عَلٰى مُحَمَّدٍ صَلَاةً تُنْجِيْنَا بِهَا مِنْ جَمِيْعِ الْأَهْوَالِ وَالْاٰفَاتِ، وَتَقْضِيْ لَنَا بِهَا جَمِيْعَ الْحَاجَاتِ، وَتُطَهِّرُنَا بِهَا مِنْ جَمِيْعِ السَّيِّئَاتِ، وَتَرْفَعُنَا بِهَا عِنْدَكَ أَعْلَى الدَّرَجَاتِ، وَتُبَلِّغُنَا بِهَا أَقْصَى الْغَايَاتِ مِنْ جَمِيْعِ الْخَيْرَاتِ فِي الْحَيَاةِ وَبَعْدَ الْمَمَاتِ، إِنَّكَ عَلٰى كُلِّ شَيْءٍ قَدِيْرٌ

50. I am present, O Allāh, my Lord, intent on aiding Your cause time and again. The blessings of Allāh, Most Kind and Merciful, and that of the intimate angels, prophets, truthful ones, martyrs, righteous, and all things that exalt You, O Lord of the Worlds, be upon Muḥammad son of ʿAbdullāh, seal of the prophets, master of the messengers, imām of the god-fearing, the Messenger of the Lord of the Worlds, the witness, giver of glad tidings, caller to You with Your permission, and the illuminating lamp; and upon him be peace.

﴿٥٠﴾ لَبَّيْكَ، اللّٰهُمَّ رَبِّيْ وَسَعْدَيْكَ، صَلَوَاتُ اللهِ الْبَرِّ الرَّحِيْمِ، وَالْمَلَائِكَةِ الْمُقَرَّبِيْنَ وَالنَّبِيِّيْنَ وَالصِّدِّيْقِيْنَ وَالشُّهَدَاءِ وَالصَّالِحِيْنَ، وَمَا سَبَّحَ لَكَ مِنْ شَيْءٍ، يَّا رَبَّ الْعَالَمِيْنَ، عَلٰى مُحَمَّدِ بْنِ عَبْدِ اللهِ خَاتَمِ النَّبِيِّيْنَ وَسَيِّدِ الْمُرْسَلِيْنَ وَإِمَامِ الْمُتَّقِيْنَ وَرَسُوْلِ رَبِّ الْعَالَمِيْنَ، الشَّاهِدِ الْبَشِيْرِ الدَّاعِيْ إِلَيْكَ بِإِذْنِكَ السِّرَاجِ الْمُنِيْرِ، وَعَلَيْهِ السَّلَامُ

محمد رسول الله

Part Two

Ninety-Nine Invocations of Blessings and Peace

with the Beautiful Names of Allāh and Prophetic Attributes

by Shaykh Yusuf ibn Sulayman Motala

In the name of Allāh, Most Beneficent, Most Merciful.

He is Allāh besides whom there is no god.

Most Beneficent! Your blessings and peace on the Prophet, the clear proof.

Most Merciful! Your blessings and peace on the Prophet most graceful.

Sovereign! Your blessings and peace on the Prophet most pious and chaste.

Most Holy! Your blessings and peace on the Prophet most purified.

Giver of Peace! Your blessings and peace on the Prophet, the haven.

Guardian of Faith! Your blessings and peace on the Prophet herald of truth.

Protector! Your blessings and peace on the Prophet, the helper.

Almighty! Your blessings and peace on the Prophet most cogent.

بِسْمِ اللهِ الرَّحْمٰنِ الرَّحِيمِ

هُوَ اللهُ الَّذِيْ لَا إِلٰهَ إِلَّا هُوْ

يَا رَحْمٰنْ، صَلِّ وَسَلِّمْ عَلَى النَّبِيِّ الْبُرْهَانْ

يَا رَحِيمْ، صَلِّ وَسَلِّمْ عَلَى النَّبِيِّ الْوَسِيمْ

يَا مَلِكْ، صَلِّ وَسَلِّمْ عَلَى النَّبِيِّ الْوَرِعْ

يَا قُدُّوسْ، صَلِّ وَسَلِّمْ عَلَى النَّبِيِّ الْمُقَدَّسْ

يَا سَلَامْ، صَلِّ وَسَلِّمْ عَلَى النَّبِيِّ الْأَمَانْ

يَا مُؤْمِنْ، صَلِّ وَسَلِّمْ عَلَى النَّبِيِّ الْمُعْلِنْ

يَا مُهَيْمِنْ، صَلِّ وَسَلِّمْ عَلَى النَّبِيِّ الْمُيَسِّرْ

يَا عَزِيزْ، صَلِّ وَسَلِّمْ عَلَى النَّبِيِّ الْمُبِينْ

Compeller! Your blessings and peace on the Prophet elect.

Glorifying Lord! Your blessings and peace on the Prophet most humble.

Creator! Your blessings and peace on the Prophet, the first light.

Maker! Your blessings and peace on the Prophet most brilliant.

Fashioner! Your blessings and peace on the Prophet, the wise counsel.

Most Forgiving! Your blessings and peace on the Prophet most grateful.

Conqueror! Your blessings and peace on the Prophet most mindful of You.

Bestower! Your blessings and peace on the Prophet most reverent.

Provider! Your blessings and peace on the Prophet most generous.

Facilitator! Your blessings and peace on the Prophet most awed.

يَا جَبَّارْ، صَلِّ وَسَلِّمْ عَلَى النَّبِيِّ الْمُخْتَارْ

يَا مُتَكَبِّرْ، صَلِّ وَسَلِّمْ عَلَى النَّبِيِّ الْمُتَضَرِّعْ

يَا خَالِقْ، صَلِّ وَسَلِّمْ عَلَى النَّبِيِّ السَّابِقْ

يَا بَارِئْ، صَلِّ وَسَلِّمْ عَلَى النَّبِيِّ الْبَارِعْ

يَا مُصَوِّرْ، صَلِّ وَسَلِّمْ عَلَى النَّبِيِّ الْمُذَكِّرْ

يَا غَفَّارْ، صَلِّ وَسَلِّمْ عَلَى النَّبِيِّ الشَّكَّارْ

يَا قَهَّارْ، صَلِّ وَسَلِّمْ عَلَى النَّبِيِّ الذَّكَّارْ

يَا وَهَّابْ، صَلِّ وَسَلِّمْ عَلَى النَّبِيِّ الرَّهَّابْ

يَا رَزَّاقْ، صَلِّ وَسَلِّمْ عَلَى النَّبِيِّ الْجَوَّادْ

يَا فَتَّاحْ، صَلِّ وَسَلِّمْ عَلَى النَّبِيِّ الْأَوَّاهْ

All-Knowing You! Your blessings and peace on the Prophet most gentle.

Constrictor! Your blessings and peace on the Prophet, distributor of Your bounty.

Expounder! Your blessings and peace on the Prophet, the witness.

Abaser! Your blessings and peace on the Prophet most needy.

Exalter! Your blessings and peace on the Prophet, the intercessor.

Honorer! Your blessings and peace on the Prophet most caring.

Giver of Disgrace! Your blessings and peace on the Prophet, the bane of evil.

All-Hearing You! Your blessings and peace on the Prophet, the intercessor.

All-Seeing You! Your blessings and peace on the Prophet, giver of glad tidings.

Absolute Judge! Your blessings and peace on the Prophet most noble.

يَا عَلِيمْ، صَلِّ وَسَلِّمْ عَلَى النَّبِيِّ الْحَلِيمْ

يَا قَابِضْ، صَلِّ وَسَلِّمْ عَلَى النَّبِيِّ الْقَاسِمْ

يَا بَاسِطْ، صَلِّ وَسَلِّمْ عَلَى النَّبِيِّ الشَّاهِدْ

يَا خَافِضْ، صَلِّ وَسَلِّمْ عَلَى النَّبِيِّ الْوَاضِعْ

يَا رَافِعْ، صَلِّ وَسَلِّمْ عَلَى النَّبِيِّ الشَّافِعْ

يَا مُعِزّ، صَلِّ وَسَلِّمْ عَلَى النَّبِيِّ الْمُعِينْ

يَا مُذِلّ، صَلِّ وَسَلِّمْ عَلَى النَّبِيِّ الْمُزِيلْ

يَا سَمِيعْ، صَلِّ وَسَلِّمْ عَلَى النَّبِيِّ الشَّفِيعْ

يَا بَصِيرْ، صَلِّ وَسَلِّمْ عَلَى النَّبِيِّ الْبَشِيرْ

يَا حَكَمْ، صَلِّ وَسَلِّمْ عَلَى النَّبِيِّ الْأَكْرَمْ

Most Just! Your blessings and peace on the Prophet, the full moon.

Knower of the Inmost Secrets! Your blessings and peace on the Prophet, the true believer.

All-Aware! Your blessings and peace on the Prophet, the forewarner.

Most Clement! Your blessings and peace on the Prophet most wise.

Most Magnificent! Your blessings and peace on the Prophet most bountiful.

All-Forgiving! Your blessings and peace on the Prophet most victorious.

You Who Acknowledges Gratitude! Your blessings and peace on the Prophet most pure.

Most High! Your blessings and peace on the Prophet most devout.

Most Great! Your blessings and peace on the Prophet most rewarded.

Protector! Your blessings and peace on the Prophet most beloved.

يَا عَدلْ، صَلِّ وَسَلِّمْ عَلَى النَّبِيِّ الْبَدرْ

يَا لَطِيفْ، صَلِّ وَسَلِّمْ عَلَى النَّبِيِّ الْحَنِيفْ

يَا خَبِيرْ، صَلِّ وَسَلِّمْ عَلَى النَّبِيِّ النَّذِيرْ

يَا حَلِيمْ، صَلِّ وَسَلِّمْ عَلَى النَّبِيِّ الْحَكِيمْ

يَا عَظِيمْ، صَلِّ وَسَلِّمْ عَلَى النَّبِيِّ الْكَرِيمْ

يَا غَفُورْ، صَلِّ وَسَلِّمْ عَلَى النَّبِيِّ الظَّفُورْ

يَا شَكُورْ، صَلِّ وَسَلِّمْ عَلَى النَّبِيِّ الطَّهُورْ

يَا عَلِيّ، صَلِّ وَسَلِّمْ عَلَى النَّبِيِّ التَّقِيّ

يَا كَبِيرْ، صَلِّ وَسَلِّمْ عَلَى النَّبِيِّ الأَجِيرْ

يَا حَفِيظْ، صَلِّ وَسَلِّمْ عَلَى النَّبِيِّ الْعَزِيزْ

Fortifier! Your blessings and peace on the Prophet most steadfast.

Reckoner! Your blessings and peace on the Prophet most noble in lineage.

Most Majestic! Your blessings and peace on the Prophet most near.

Most Benevolent! Your blessings and peace on the Prophet most gentle.

Most Vigilant! Your blessings and peace on the Prophet most dear.

Answerer of Prayers! Your blessings and peace on the Prophet oft-returning.

Most Amply Giving! Your blessings and peace on the Prophet most fearful.

Most Wise! Your blessings and peace on the Prophet, the master.

Most Loving! Your blessings and peace on the Prophet, the night vigilant.

Most Venerable! Your blessings and peace on the Prophet most fortunate.

يَا مُقِيتْ، صَلِّ وَسَلِّمْ عَلَى النَّبِيِّ الْمُقِيمْ

يَا حَسِيبْ، صَلِّ وَسَلِّمْ عَلَى النَّبِيِّ النَّسِيبْ

يَا جَلِيلْ، صَلِّ وَسَلِّمْ عَلَى النَّبِيِّ الْخَلِيلْ

يَا كَرِيمْ، صَلِّ وَسَلِّمْ عَلَى النَّبِيِّ الرَّحِيمْ

يَا رَقِيبْ، صَلِّ وَسَلِّمْ عَلَى النَّبِيِّ الْحَبِيبْ

يَا مُجِيبْ، صَلِّ وَسَلِّمْ عَلَى النَّبِيِّ الْمُنِيبْ

يَا وَاسِعْ، صَلِّ وَسَلِّمْ عَلَى النَّبِيِّ الْخَاشِعْ

يَا حَكِيمْ، صَلِّ وَسَلِّمْ عَلَى النَّبِيِّ الزَّعِيمْ

يَا وَدُودْ، صَلِّ وَسَلِّمْ عَلَى النَّبِيِّ الْهَجُودْ

يَا مَجِيدْ، صَلِّ وَسَلِّمْ عَلَى النَّبِيِّ السَّعِيدْ

Resurrector! Your blessings and peace on the Prophet, most desiring of the Hereafter.

Witness to All! Your blessings and peace on the Prophet most guided.

Most True! Your blessings and peace on the Prophet most truthful.

Keeper! Your blessings and peace on the Prophet most eminent.

Powerful! Your blessings and peace on the Prophet most preferred.

Most Firm! Your blessings and peace on the Prophet most trusted.

Patron! Your blessings and peace on the Prophet most faithful.

Most Praiseworthy! Your blessings and peace on the Prophet, pursuer of the right course.

Recorder! Your blessings and peace on the Prophet, the exalter.

Originator! Your blessings and peace on the Prophet, teacher of the Qur'ān.

يَا بَاعِثْ، صَلِّ وَسَلِّمْ عَلَى النَّبِيِّ الرَّاغِبْ

يَا شَهِيدْ، صَلِّ وَسَلِّمْ عَلَى النَّبِيِّ الرَّشِيدْ

يَا حَقّ، صَلِّ وَسَلِّمْ عَلَى النَّبِيِّ الْأَصْدَقْ

يَا وَكِيلْ، صَلِّ وَسَلِّمْ عَلَى النَّبِيِّ الْجَلِيلْ

يَا قَوِيّ، صَلِّ وَسَلِّمْ عَلَى النَّبِيِّ الصَّفِيّ

يَا مَتِينْ، صَلِّ وَسَلِّمْ عَلَى النَّبِيِّ الْأَمِينْ

يَا وَلِيّ، صَلِّ وَسَلِّمْ عَلَى النَّبِيِّ الْوَفِيّ

يَا حَمِيدْ، صَلِّ وَسَلِّمْ عَلَى النَّبِيِّ السَّدِيدْ

يَا مُحْصِيْ، صَلِّ وَسَلِّمْ عَلَى النَّبِيِّ الْمُعْلِيْ

يَا مُبْدِئْ، صَلِّ وَسَلِّمْ عَلَى النَّبِيِّ الْمُقْرِئْ

Restorer! Your blessings and peace on the Prophet who renounces falsehood.

Giver of Life! Your blessings and peace on the unlettered Prophet.

Giver of Death! Your blessings and peace on the illuminating Prophet.

Ever-Living! Your blessings and peace on the good Prophet.

Self-Subsistent! Your blessings and peace on the Prophet most divinely aided.

Resourceful You! Your blessings and peace on the Prophet, the promise keeper.

Most August! Your blessings and peace on the Prophet most ardent in worship.

Peerless You! Your blessings and peace on the Prophet, the leader.

Incomparable You! Your blessings and peace on the Prophet, the brilliant moon.

You Free of Want! Your blessings and peace on the Prophet, the best of men.

يَا مُعِيدْ، صَلِّ وَسَلِّمْ عَلَى النَّبِيِّ الْمُحِيدْ

يَا مُحْيِيْ، صَلِّ وَسَلِّمْ عَلَى النَّبِيِّ الْأُمِّيّ

يَا مُمِيتْ، صَلِّ وَسَلِّمْ عَلَى النَّبِيِّ الْمُنِيرْ

يَا حَيّ، صَلِّ وَسَلِّمْ عَلَى النَّبِيِّ الْخَيرْ

يَا قَيُّومْ، صَلِّ وَسَلِّمْ عَلَى النَّبِيِّ الْمَنْصُورْ

يَا وَاجِدْ، صَلِّ وَسَلِّمْ عَلَى النَّبِيِّ الْوَاعِدْ

يَا مَاجِدْ، صَلِّ وَسَلِّمْ عَلَى النَّبِيِّ الْعَابِدْ

يَا وَاحِدْ، صَلِّ وَسَلِّمْ عَلَى النَّبِيِّ الْقَائِدْ

يَا أَحَدْ، صَلِّ وَسَلِّمْ عَلَى النَّبِيِّ الْقَمَرْ

يَا صَمَدْ، صَلِّ وَسَلِّمْ عَلَى النَّبِيِّ الْبَشَرْ

All-Powerful You! Your blessings and peace on the Prophet most grateful.

You with Full-Authority! Your blessings and peace on the Prophet most temperate.

Advancer! Your blessings and peace on the Prophet, the foremost.

Postponer! Your blessings and peace on the Prophet bearer of good news.

The First! Your blessings and peace on the Prophet most handsome.

The Last! Your blessings and peace on the Prophet most glorifying.

The Manifest! Your blessings and peace on the Prophet most evident.

The Hidden! Your blessings and peace on the Prophet free from fear.

Supreme Ruler! Your blessings and peace on the Prophet most hopeful.

Most Exalted! Your blessings and peace on the Prophet, reciter of his Lord's praise.

يَا قَادِرْ، صَلِّ وَسَلِّمْ عَلَى النَّبِيِّ الشَّاكِرْ

يَا مُقْتَدِرْ، صَلِّ وَسَلِّمْ عَلَى النَّبِيِّ الْمُقْتَصِدْ

يَا مُقَدِّمْ، صَلِّ وَسَلِّمْ عَلَى النَّبِيِّ الْمُقَدَّمْ

يَا مُؤَخِّرْ، صَلِّ وَسَلِّمْ عَلَى النَّبِيِّ الْمُبَشِّرْ

يَا أَوَّلْ، صَلِّ وَسَلِّمْ عَلَى النَّبِيِّ الأَجْمَلْ

يَا أٰخِرْ، صَلِّ وَسَلِّمْ عَلَى النَّبِيِّ الذَّاكِرْ

يَا ظَاهِرْ، صَلِّ وَسَلِّمْ عَلَى النَّبِيِّ الزَّاهِرْ

يَا بَاطِنْ، صَلِّ وَسَلِّمْ عَلَى النَّبِيِّ الْأٰمِنْ

يَا وَالِيْ، صَلِّ وَسَلِّمْ عَلَى النَّبِيِّ الرَّاجِيْ

يَا مُتَعَالِيْ، صَلِّ وَسَلِّمْ عَلَى النَّبِيِّ التَّالِيْ

Most Kind! Your blessings and peace on the Prophet, the ocean of kindness.

Most Forbearing! Your blessings and peace on the Prophet, most frequent in praise.

Avenger! Your blessings and peace on the Prophet, most meek in prayer.

Pardoner! Your blessings and peace on the Prophet most celebrated.

Most Loving! Your blessings and peace on the Prophet most affectionate.

Lord of Realms! Your blessings and peace on the Prophet, standard-bearer of praise.

Lord of Majesty and Goodwill! Your blessings and peace on the Prophet of guidance, most fair.

Most Just! Your blessings and peace on the Prophet, the reformer of men.

Assembler! Your blessings and peace on the Prophet most dutiful.

You Free from Want! Your blessings and peace on the Prophet most openhanded.

يَا بَرّ، صَلِّ وَسَلِّمْ عَلَى النَّبِيِّ الْبَحرْ

يَا تَوَّابْ، صَلِّ وَسَلِّمْ عَلَى النَّبِيِّ الْحَمَّادْ

يَا مُنْتَقِمْ، صَلِّ وَسَلِّمْ عَلَى النَّبِيِّ الْمُبْتَهِلْ

يَا عَفُوّ، صَلِّ وَسَلِّمْ عَلَى النَّبِيِّ الْمَتْلُوّ

يَا رَؤُوفْ، صَلِّ وَسَلِّمْ عَلَى النَّبِيِّ الْعَطُوفْ

يَا مَالِكَ الْمُلكْ، صَلِّ وَسَلِّمْ عَلَى النَّبِيِّ حَامِلِ لِوَاءِ الْحَمدْ

يَا ذَا لْجَلَالِ وَالْإِكْرَامْ، صَلِّ وَسَلِّمْ عَلَى النَّبِيِّ الْهُدٰى وَالْهُمَامْ

يَا مُقْسِطْ، صَلِّ وَسَلِّمْ عَلَى النَّبِيِّ الْمُصْلِحْ

يَا جَامِعْ، صَلِّ وَسَلِّمْ عَلَى النَّبِيِّ الْخَاضِعْ

يَا غَنِيّ، صَلِّ وَسَلِّمْ عَلَى النَّبِيِّ السَّخِيّ

Enricher! Your blessings and peace on the Prophet, the guide.

Proscriber! Your blessings and peace on the Prophet, the legislator.

Upsetter! Your blessings and peace on the Prophet, who turns evil from his people.

Benefactor! Your blessings and peace on the Prophet most upright.

Light! Your blessings and peace on the Prophet, the pure spirit.

Guide! Your blessings and peace on the Prophet, the healer.

Deviser! Your blessings and peace on the Prophet possessed of light.

Everlasting! Your blessings and peace on the Prophet who roots out unbelief.

Inheritor! Your blessings and peace on the Prophet most ascendant.

Lover of Virtue! Your blessings and peace on the Prophet, the brave.

Enduring You! Your blessings and peace on the Prophet, the grateful.

يَا مُغْنِيْ، صَلِّ وَسَلِّمْ عَلَى النَّبِيِّ الْمُهْدِيْ

يَا مَانِعْ، صَلِّ وَسَلِّمْ عَلَى النَّبِيِّ الشَّارِعْ

يَا ضَارّ، صَلِّ وَسَلِّمْ عَلَى النَّبِيِّ الْكَافّ

يَا نَافِعْ، صَلِّ وَسَلِّمْ عَلَى النَّبِيِّ الصَّالِحْ

يَا نُورْ، صَلِّ وَسَلِّمْ عَلَى النَّبِيِّ الرُّوحْ

يَا هَادِيْ، صَلِّ وَسَلِّمْ عَلَى النَّبِيِّ الشَّافِيْ

يَا بَدِيعْ، صَلِّ وَسَلِّمْ عَلَى النَّبِيِّ الْبَهِيّ

يَا بَاقِيْ، صَلِّ وَسَلِّمْ عَلَى النَّبِيِّ الْمَاحِيْ

يَا وَارِثْ، صَلِّ وَسَلِّمْ عَلَى النَّبِيِّ الْغَالِبْ

يَا رَشِيدْ، صَلِّ وَسَلِّمْ عَلَى النَّبِيِّ النَّجِيدْ

يَا صَبُورْ، صَلِّ وَسَلِّمْ عَلَى النَّبِيِّ الشَّكُورْ

Transliteration

Fifty Invocations of Blessings and Peace

Bismi 'Llāhi 'r-Raḥmān al-Raḥīm.

Salāmun ᶜalā ᶜibādihi 'lladhīna 'ṣṭafā. Salāmun ᶜala 'l-mursalīn(a).

1. Allāhumma ṣalli ᶜalā Muḥammadiw wa ᶜalā āli Muḥammadiw wa anzilhu 'l-maqᶜada 'l-muqarraba ᶜindak(a).

2. Allāhumma Rabba hādhihi 'd-daᶜwati 'l-qā'imati wa 'ṣ-ṣalāti 'n-nāfi-ᶜati ṣalli ᶜalā Muḥammadiw wa 'rḍa ᶜannī riḍal lā taskhaṭu baᶜdahū abadan.

3. Allāhumma ṣalli ᶜalā Muḥammadin ᶜabdika wa rasūlika wa ṣalli ᶜala 'l-mu'minīna wa 'l-mu'mināti wa 'l-muslimīna wa 'l-muslimāt(i).

4. Allāhumma ṣalli ᶜalā Muḥammadiw wa ᶜalā āli Muḥammadiw wa bārik ᶜalā Muḥammadiw wa ᶜalā āli Muḥammadiw wa 'rḥam Muḥammadaw wa āla Muḥammadin kamā ṣallayta wa bārakta wa raḥimta ᶜalā Ibrāhīma wa ᶜalā āli Ibrāhīm(a), innaka ḥamīdum majīd(un).

5. Allāhumma ṣalli ʿalā Muḥammadiw wa ʿalā āli Muḥammadin kamā ṣallayta ʿalā āli Ibrāhīm(a), innaka ḥamīdum majīd(un). Allāhumma bārik ʿalā Muḥammadiw wa ʿalā āli Muḥammadin kamā bārakta ʿalā āli Ibrāhīm(a), innaka ḥamīdum majīd(un).

6. Allāhumma ṣalli ʿalā Muḥammadiw wa ʿalā āli Muḥammadin kamā ṣallayta ʿalā āli Ibrāhīm(a), innaka ḥamīdum majīd(un), wa bārik ʿalā Muḥammadiw wa ʿalā āli Muḥammadin kamā bārakta ʿalā āli Ibrāhīm(a), innaka ḥamīdum majīd(un).

7. Allāhumma ṣalli ʿalā Muḥammadiw wa ʿalā āli Muḥammadin kamā ṣallayta ʿalā Ibrāhīm(a), innaka ḥamīdum majīd(un). Allāhumma bārik ʿalā Muḥammadiw wa ʿalā āli Muḥammadin kamā bārakta ʿalā Ibrāhīm(a), innaka ḥamīdum majīd(un).

8. Allāhumma ṣalli ʿalā Muḥammadiw wa ʿalā āli Muḥammadin kamā ṣallayta ʿalā Ibrāhīma wa ʿalā āli Ibrāhīm(a), innaka ḥamīdum majīd(un), wa bārik ʿalā Muḥammadiw wa ʿalā āli Muḥammadin kamā bārakta ʿalā Ibrāhīm(a), innaka ḥamīdum majīd(un).

9. Allāhumma ṣalli ʿalā Muḥammadiw wa ʿalā āli Muḥammadin kamā ṣallayta ʿalā Ibrāhīma wa bārik ʿalā Muḥammadiw wa ʿalā āli Muḥammadin kamā bārakta ʿalā Ibrāhīm(a), innaka ḥamīdum majīd(un).

10. Allāhumma ṣalli ʿalā Muḥammadiw wa ʿalā āli Muḥammadin kamā ṣallayta ʿalā Ibrāhīm(a), innaka ḥamīdum majīd(un). Allāhumma bārik ʿalā Muḥammadiw wa ʿalā āli Muḥammadin

kamā bārakta ʿalā āli Ibrāhīm(a), innaka ḥamīdum majīd(un).

11. Allāhumma ṣalli ʿalā Muḥammadiw wa ʿalā āli Muḥammadin kamā ṣallayta ʿalā āli Ibrāhīma wa bārik ʿalā Muḥammadiw wa ʿalā āli Muḥammadin kamā bārakta ʿalā āli Ibrāhīma fi 'l-ʿālamīn(a), innaka ḥamīdum majīd(un).

12. Allāhumma ṣalli ʿalā Muḥammadiw wa azwājihī wa dhurriyyatihī kamā ṣallayta ʿalā āli Ibrāhīma wa bārik ʿalā Muḥammadiw wa azwājihī wa dhurriyyatihī kamā bārakta ʿalā āli Ibrāhīm(a), innaka ḥamīdum majīd(un).

13. Allāhumma ṣalli ʿalā Muḥammadiw wa ʿalā azwājihī wa dhurriyyatihī kamā ṣallayta ʿalā āli Ibrāhīma wa bārik ʿalā Muḥammadiw wa ʿalā azwājihī wa dhurriyyatihī kamā bārakta ʿalā āli Ibrāhīm(a), innaka ḥamīdum majīd(un).

14. Allāhumma ṣalli ʿalā Muḥammadini 'n-nabiyyi wa azwājihī ummahāti 'l-mu'minīna wa dhurriyyatihī wa ahli baytihī kamā ṣallayta ʿalā Ibrāhīm(a), innaka ḥamīdum majīd(un).

15. Allāhumma ṣalli ʿalā Muḥammadiw wa ʿalā āli Muḥammadin kamā ṣallayta ʿalā Ibrāhīma wa ʿalā āli Ibrāhīm(a), wa bārik ʿalā Muḥammadiw wa ʿalā āli Muḥammadin kamā bārakta ʿalā Ibrāhīm(a), wa taraḥḥam ʿalā Muḥammadiw wa ʿalā āli Muḥammadin kamā taraḥḥamta ʿalā Ibrāhīma wa ʿalā āli Ibrāhīm(a).

16. Allāhumma ṣalli ʿalā Muḥammadiw wa ʿalā āli Muḥammadin kamā ṣallayta ʿalā Ibrāhīma wa ʿalā āli Ibrāhīm(a), innaka

ḥamīdum majīd(un). Allāhumma bārik ʿalā Muḥammadiw wa ʿalā āli Muḥammadin kamā bārakta ʿalā Ibrāhīma wa ʿalā āli Ibrāhīm(a), innaka ḥamīdum majīd(un). Allāhumma taraḥḥam ʿalā Muḥammadiw wa ʿalā āli Muḥammadin kamā taraḥḥamta ʿalā Ibrāhīma wa ʿalā āli Ibrāhīm(a), innaka ḥamīdum majīd(un). Allāhumma taḥannan ʿalā Muḥammadiw wa ʿalā āli Muḥammadin kamā taḥannanta ʿalā Ibrāhīma wa ʿalā āli Ibrāhīm(a), innaka ḥamīdum majīd(un). Allāhumma sallim ʿalā Muḥammadiw wa ʿalā āli Muḥammadin kamā sallamta ʿalā Ibrāhīma wa ʿalā āli Ibrāhīm(a), innaka ḥamīdum majīd(un).

17. Allāhumma ṣalli ʿalā Muḥammadiw wa ʿalā āli Muḥammad(iw), wa bārik wa sallim ʿalā Muḥammadiw wa ʿalā āli Muḥammad(iw), wa ʾrḥam Muḥammadaw wa āla Muḥammadin kamā ṣallayta wa bārakta wa taraḥḥamta ʿalā Ibrāhīma wa ʿalā āli Ibrāhīma fi ʾl-ʿālamīn(a), innaka ḥamīdum majīd(un).

18. Allāhumma ṣalli ʿalā Muḥammadiw wa ʿalā āli Muḥammadin kamā ṣallayta ʿalā Ibrāhīma wa ʿalā āli Ibrāhīm(a), innaka ḥamīdum majīd(un). Allāhumma bārik ʿalā Muḥammadiw wa ʿalā āli Muḥammadin kamā bārakta ʿalā Ibrāhīma wa ʿalā āli Ibrāhīm(a), innaka ḥamīdum majīd(un).

19. Allāhumma ṣalli ʿalā Muḥammadin ʿabdika wa rasūlika kamā ṣallayta ʿalā āli Ibrāhīm(a), wa bārik ʿalā Muḥammadiw wa ʿalā āli Muḥammadin kamā bārakta ʿalā āli Ibrahīm(a)

20. Allāhumma ṣalli ʿalā Muḥammadini ʾn-nabiyyi ʾl-ummiyyi wa

ʿalā āli Muḥammadin kamā ṣallayta ʿalā Ibrāhīma, wa bārik ʿalā Muḥammadini ʼn-nabiyyi ʼl-ummiyyi kamā bārakta ʿalā Ibrāhīm(a), innaka ḥamīdum majīd(un).

21. Allāhumma ṣalli ʿalā Muḥammadin ʿabdika wa rasūlika ʼn-nabiyyi ʼl-ummiyyi wa ʿalā āli Muḥammad(in). Allāhumma ṣalli ʿalā Muḥammadin wa ʿalā āli Muḥammadin ṣalātan takūnu laka riḍaw wa lahū jazāʾaw wa li ḥaqqihī adāʾaw, wa aʿṭihi ʼl-wasīlata wa l-faḍīlata wa ʼl-maqāma ʼl-maḥmūda ʼlladhī wa-ʿattah(ū), wa ʼjzihī ʿannā mā huwa ahluh(ū), wa ʼjzihī afḍala mā jāzayta nabiyyan ʿan qawmihī wa rasūlan ʿan ummatih(ī), wa ṣalli ʿalā jamī-ʿi ikhwānihī mina ʼn-nabiyyīna wa ʼṣ-ṣāliḥīn(a), yā Arḥama ʼr-rāḥimīn(a).

22. Allāhumma ṣalli ʿalā Muḥammadini ʼn-nabiyyi ʼl-ummiyyi wa ʿalā āli Muḥammadin kamā ṣallayta ʿalā Ibrāhīma wa ʿalā āli Ibrāhīm(a), wa bārik ʿalā Muḥammadini ʼn-nabiyyi ʼl-ummiyyi wa ʿalā āli Muḥammadin kamā bārakta ʿalā Ibrāhīma wa ʿalā āli Ibrāhīm(a), innaka ḥamīdum majīd(un).

23. Allāhumma ṣalli ʿalā Muḥammadiw wa ʿalā ahli baytihī kamā ṣallayta ʿalā Ibrāhīm(a), innaka ḥamīdum majīd(un). Allāhumma ṣalli ʿalaynā ma-ʿahum. Allāhumma bārik ʿalā Muḥammadiw wa ʿalā ahli baytihī kamā bārakta ʿalā Ibrāhīm(a), innaka ḥamīdum majīd(un). Allāhumma bārik ʿalaynā ma-ʿahum. Ṣalawātu ʼLlāhi wa ṣalawātu ʼl-muʼminīna ʿalā Muḥammadini ʼn-nabiyyi ʼl-ummiyy(i).

24. Allāhumma ʼjʿal ṣalawātika wa raḥmataka wa barakātika ʿalā Muḥammadiw wa ʿalā āli Muḥammadin kamā ja-ʿaltahā

ʿalā āli Ibrāhīm(a), innaka ḥamīdum majīd(un), wa bārik ʿalā Muḥammadiw wa ʿalā āli Muḥammadin kamā bārakta ʿalā Ibrāhīma wa ʿalā āli Ibrāhīm(a), innaka ḥamīdum majīd(un).

25. Wa ṣalla 'Llāhu ʿala 'n-nabiyyi 'l-ummiyy(i).

26. At-taḥiyyātu li 'Llāhi wa 'ṣ-ṣalawātu wa 'ṭ-ṭayyibāt(u), 's-salāmu ʿalayka ayyuha 'n-nabiyyu wa raḥmatu 'Llāhi wa barakātuh(ū), 's-salāmu ʿalaynā wa ʿalā ʿibādi 'Llāhi 'ṣ-ṣāliḥīn(a). Ashhadu al lā ilāha illa 'Llāhu wa ashhadu anna Muḥammadan ʿabduhū wa rasūluh(ū).

27. At-taḥiyyātu 'ṭ-ṭayyibātu 'ṣ-ṣalawātu li 'Llāh(i), 's-salāmu ʿalayka ayyuha 'n-nabiyyu wa raḥmatu 'Llāhi wa barakātuh(ū), 's-salāmu ʿalaynā wa ʿalā ʿibādi 'Llāhi 'ṣ-ṣāliḥīn(a). Ashhadu al lā ilāha illa 'Llāhu wa ashhadu anna Muḥammadan ʿabduhū wa rasūluh(ū).

28. At-taḥiyyātu li 'Llāhi 'ṭ-ṭayyibātu 'ṣ-ṣalawātu li 'Llāh(i), 's-salāmu ʿalayka ayyuha 'n-nabiyyu wa raḥmatu 'Llāhi wa barakātuh(ū), 's-salāmu ʿalaynā wa ʿalā ʿibādi 'Llāhi 'ṣ-ṣāliḥīn(a). Ashhadu al lā ilāha illa 'Llāhu waḥdahū lā sharīka lahū wa ashhadu anna Muḥammadan ʿabduhū wa rasūluh(ū).

29. At-taḥiyyātu 'l-mubārakātu 'ṣ-ṣalawātu 'ṭ-ṭayyibātu li 'Llāh(i), salāmun ʿalayka ayyuha 'n-nabiyyu wa raḥmatu 'Llāhi wa barakātuh(ū), salāmun ʿalaynā wa ʿalā ʿibādi 'Llāhi 'ṣ-ṣāliḥīn(a). Ashhadu al lā ilāha illa 'Llāhu wa ashhadu anna Muḥammadan ʿabduhū wa rasūluh(ū).

30. Bismillāhi wa bi 'Llāh(i), (a)'t-taḥiyyātu li 'Llāh(i), wa 'ṣ-

ṣalawātu wa 'ṭ-ṭayyibāt(u), 's-salāmu ʿayyuha 'n-nabiyyu wa raḥmatu 'Llāhi wa barakātuh(ū), 's-salāmu ʿalaynā wa ʿalā ʿibādi 'Llāhi 'ṣ-ṣāliḥīn(a). Ashhadu al lā ilāha illa 'Llāhu wa ashhadu anna Muḥammadan ʿabduhū wa rasūluh(ū). As'alu 'Llāha 'l-jannata wa a-ʿūdhu bi 'Llāhi mina 'n-nar(i).

31. At-taḥiyyātu li 'Llāhi 'z-zākiyātu li 'Llāhi 'ṭ-ṭayyibātu 'ṣ-ṣalawātu li 'Llāh(i), 's-salāmu ʿalayka ayyuha 'n-nabiyyu wa raḥmatu 'Llāhi wa barakātuh(ū), 's-salāmu ʿalaynā wa ʿalā ʿibādi 'Llāhi 'ṣ-ṣāliḥīn(a). Ashhadu al lā ilāha illa 'Llāhu wa ashhadu anna Muḥammadan ʿabduhū wa rasūluh(ū).

32. Bismillāhi wa bi 'Llāhi khayri 'l-asmā'i 't-taḥiyyātu 'ṭ-ṭayyibātu 'ṣ-ṣalawātu li 'Llāh(i). Ashhadu al lā ilāha illa 'Llāhu waḥdahū lā sharīka lahū wa ashhadu anna Muḥammadan ʿabduhū wa rasūluh(ū), arsalahū bi 'l-ḥaqqi bashīraw wa nadhīraw wa anna 's-sā-ʿata 'ātiyatul lā rayba fīhā. As-salāmu ʿalayka ayyuha 'n-nabiyyu wa raḥmatu 'Llāhi wa barakātuh(ū), (a)'s-salāmu ʿalaynā wa ʿalā ʿibādi 'Llāhi 'ṣ-ṣāliḥīn(a). Allāhumma 'ghfir lī wa 'hdinī.

33. At-taḥiyyātu 'ṭ-ṭayyibātu wa 'ṣ-ṣalawātu wa 'l-mulku li 'Llāh(i), 's-salāmu ʿalayka ayyuha 'n-nabiyyu wa raḥmatu 'Llāhi wa barakātuh(ū).

34. Bismi 'Llāh(i), 't-taḥiyyātu li 'Llāhi 'ṣ-ṣalawātu li 'Llāhi 'z-zākiyātu li 'Llāh(i), 's-salāmu ʿāla 'n-nabiyyi wa raḥmatu 'Llāhi wa barakātuh(ū), 's-salāmu ʿalaynā wa ʿalā ʿibādi 'Llāhi 'ṣ-ṣāliḥīn(a). Shahittu al lā ilāha illa 'Llāh(u), shahittu anna Muḥammadar rasūlu 'Llāh(i).

35. At-taḥiyyātu 'ṭ-ṭayyibātu 'ṣ-ṣalawātu 'z-zākiyātu li 'Llāh(i). Ashhadu al lā ilāha illa 'Llāhu waḥdahū lā sharīka lahū wa anna Muḥammadan ʿabduhū wa rasūluh(ū), 's-salāmu ʿalayka ayyuha 'n-nabiyyu wa raḥmatu 'Llāhi wa barakātuh(ū), 's-salāmu ʿalaynā wa ʿalā ʿibādi 'Llāhi 'ṣ-ṣāliḥīn(a).

36. At-taḥiyyātu 'ṭ-ṭayyibātu 'ṣ-ṣalawātu 'z-zākiyātu li 'Llāh(i). Ashhadu al lā ilāha illa 'Llāhu wa ashhadu anna Muḥammadan ʿabdu 'Llāhi wa rasūluh(ū). As-salāmu ʿalayka ayyuha 'n-nabiyyu wa raḥmatu 'Llāhi wa barakātuh(ū), 's-salāmu ʿalaynā wa ʿalā ʿibādi 'Llāhi 'ṣ-ṣāliḥīn(a).

37. At-taḥiyyātu 'ṣ-ṣalawātu li 'Llāh(i), 's-salāmu ʿalayka ayyuha 'n-nabiyyu wa raḥmatu 'Llāhi wa barakātuh(ū), 's-salāmu ʿalaynā wa ʿalā ʿibādi 'Llāhi 'ṣ-ṣāliḥīn(a).

38. At-taḥiyyātu li 'Llāhi 'ṣ-ṣalawātu 'ṭ-ṭayyibāt(u), 's-salāmu ʿalayka ayyuha 'n-nabiyyu wa raḥmatu 'Llāh(i), 's-salāmu ʿalaynā wa ʿalā ʿibādi 'Llāhi 'ṣ-ṣāliḥīn(a). Ashhadu al lā ilāha illa 'Llāhu wa ashhadu anna Muḥammadan ʿabduhū wa rasūluh(ū).

39. At-taḥiyyātu 'l-mubārakātu 'ṣ-ṣalawātu 'ṭ-ṭayyibātu li 'Llāh(i), 's-salāmu ʿalayka ayyuha 'n-nabiyyu wa raḥmatu 'Llāhi wa barakātuh(ū), 's-salāmu ʿalaynā wa ʿalā ʿibādi 'Llāhi 'ṣ-ṣāliḥīn(a). Ashhadu al lā ilāha illa 'Llāhu wa ashhadu anna Muḥammadar rasūlu 'Llāh(i).

40. Bismi 'Llāhi wa 's-salāmu ʿalā rasūli 'Llāh(i).

41. Allāhumma ṣalli ʿalā rūḥi Muḥammadin fi 'l-arwāḥ(i), wa ṣalli ʿalā jasadi Muḥammadin fi 'l-ajsād(i), wa ṣalli ʿalā qabri Muḥammadin fi 'l-qubūr(i).

42. Allāhumma ṣalli ʿalā Muḥammadin ḥattā lā yabqā min ṣalawātika shay'(un), wa bārik ʿalā Muḥammadin ḥattā lā yabqā mim barakātika shay'(un), wa sallim ʿalā Muḥammadin ḥattā lā yabqā min salāmika shay'(un).

43. Allāhumma ṣalli ʿalā Muḥammadim mil'a 'd-dunyā wa mil'a 'l-ākhira(ti), wa bārik ʿalā Muḥammadim mil'a 'd-dunyā wa mil'a 'l-ākhira(ti), wa 'rḥam Muḥammadam mil'a 'd-dunyā wa mil'a 'l-ākhira(ti), wa sallim ʿalā Muḥammadim mil'a 'd-dunyā wa mil'a 'l-ākhira(ti).

44. Allāhumma ṣalli ʿalā sayyidinā Muḥammadini 's-sābiqi li 'l-khalqi nūruh(ū), wa 'r-raḥmati li 'l-ʿālamīna ẓuhūruh(ū), ʿadada mam maḍā min khalqika wa mam baqiya, wa man sa-ʿida minhum wa man shaqiya, ṣalātan tastaghriqu 'l-ʿadda wa tuḥīṭu bi 'l-ḥadd(i), ṣalātal lā ghāyata lahā wa la 'ntihā'(a), wa lā amada lahā wa la 'nqiḍā'(a), ṣalātan dā'imatam bi dawāmik(a), wa ʿalā ālihī wa ṣaḥbihī kadhālik(a). Wa 'l-ḥamdu li 'Llāhi ʿalā dhālik(a).

45. Allāhumma taqabbal shafā-ʿata Muḥammadini 'l-kubrā, wa 'rfaʿ darajatahu 'l-ʿulyā, wa aʿṭihī su'lahū fi 'l-ākhirati wa 'l-ūlā, kamā ātayta Ibrāhīma wa Mūsā.

46. Allāhumma ṣalli ʿalā Muḥammadin ʿadada man ṣallā ʿalayh(i),

wa ṣalli ʿalā Muḥammadim bi ʿadadi mal lam yuṣalli ʿalayh(i), wa ṣalli ʿalā Muḥammadin kamā amarta ay yuṣallā ʿalayh(i), wa ṣalli ʿalā Muḥammadin kamā yuḥibbu ay yuṣallā ʿalayh(i), wa ṣalli ʿalā Muḥammadin kamā tanbaghi 'ṣ-ṣalātu ʿalayh(i).

47. Allāhumma innī as'aluka, yā Allāh(u), yā Raḥmān(u), yā Raḥīm(u), yā Jāra 'l-mustajīrīn(a), yā Amāna 'l-khā'ifīn(a), yā ʿImāda mal lā ʿimāda lah(ū), yā Sanada mal lā sanada lah(ū), yā Dhukhra mal lā dhukhra lah(ū), ya Ḥirza 'ḍ-ḍu-ʿafā'(i), yā Kanz al-fuqarā'(i), yā ʿAẓīma 'r-rajā'(i), yā Munqi-dha 'l-halkā, ya Munji 'l-gharqā', yā Muḥsin(u), yā Mujmil(u), yā Munʿim(u), yā Mufḍil(u), yā ʿAzīz(u), yā Jabbār(u), yā Munīr(u), Anta 'lladhī sajada laka sawādu 'l-layli wa ḍaw'u 'n-nahār(i), wa shu-ʿā'u 'sh-shams(i), wa khafīqu 'sh-shajar(i), wa dawiyyu 'l-mā'(i), wa nūru 'l-qamar(i). Yā Allāh(u), Anta 'Llāhu lā sharīka lak(a), as-'aluka an tuṣalli ʿalā Muḥammadin ʿabdika wa rasūlika wa ʿalā āli Muḥammad(in).

48. Allāhumma ṣalli ʿalā Muḥammadiw wa ʿalā āli Muḥammadiw wa aṣḥābihī wa awlādihī wa ahli baytihī wa dhurriyyatihī wa muḥibbīhi wa atbā-ʿihī wa ashyā-ʿihī, wa ʿalaynā ma-ʿahum ajma-ʿīna, yā Arḥama 'r-rāḥimīn(a).

49. Allāhumma ṣalli ʿalā Muḥammadin ṣalātan tunjīnā bihā min jamī-ʿi 'l-ahwāli wa 'l-āfāt(i), wa taqḍī lanā bihā jamī-ʿa 'l-ḥājāt(i), wa tuṭahhirunā bihā min jamī-ʿi 's-sayyi'āt(i), wa tarfa-ʿunā bihā ʿindaka aʿla 'd-darajāt(i), wa tuballighunā bihā aqṣa 'l-ghāyāti min jamī-ʿi 'l-khayrāti fi 'l-ḥayāti wa baʿda 'l-mamāt(i), innaka ʿalā kulli shay'in qadīr(un).

50. Labbayk(a), 'Llāhumma Rabbī wa saᶜdayk(a). Ṣālawātu 'Llāhi 'l-Barri 'r-Raḥīm(i), wa 'l-malā'ikati 'l-muqarrabīna wa 'n-nabiyyīna wa 'ṣ-ṣiddīqīna wa 'shshu-hadā'i wa 'ṣ-ṣāliḥīn(a), wa mā sabbaḥa laka min shay'(iy), yā Rabba 'l-ᶜālamīn(a), ᶜalā Muḥammadi 'bni ᶜAbdi 'Llāhi khātami 'n-nabiyyīna wa sayyidi 'l-murasalīna wa imāmi 'l-muttaqīna wa rasūli Rabbi 'l-ᶜālamīn(a), 'sh-shāhidi 'l-bashīr 'd-dā-ᶜī ilayka bi idhnika 's-sirāji 'l-munīr(i), wa ᶜalayhi 's-salām(u).

Ninety-Nine Invocations of Blessings and Peace

Yā Raḥmān, ṣalli wa sallim ʿala 'n-nabiyyi 'l-burhān.

Yā Raḥīm, ṣalli wa sallim ʿala 'n-nabiyyi 'l-wasīm.

Ya Malik, ṣalli wa sallim ʿala 'n-nabiyyi 'l-wariʿ.

Ya Quddūs, ṣalli wa sallim ʿala 'n-nabiyyi 'l-muqaddas.

Yā Salām, ṣalli wa sallim ʿala 'n-nabiyyi 'l-amān.

Yā Mu'min, ṣalli wa sallim ʿala 'n-nabiyyi 'l-muʿlin.

Yā Muhaymin, ṣalli wa sallim ʿala 'n-nabiyyi 'l-muyassir.

Yā ʿAzīz, ṣalli wa sallim ʿala 'n-nabiyyi 'l-mubīn.

Yā Jabbār, ṣalli wa sallim ʿala 'n-nabiyyi 'l-mukhtār.

Yā Mutakabbir, ṣalli wa sallim ʿala 'n-nabiyyi 'l-mutaḍarriʿ.

Yā Khāliq, ṣalli wa sallim ʿala 'n-nabiyyi 's-sābiq.

Yā Bāri', ṣalli wa sallim ʿala 'n-nabiyyi 'l-bāriʿ.

Yā Muṣawwir, ṣalli wa sallim ʿala 'n-nabiyyi 'l-mudhakkir.

Yā Ghaffār, ṣalli wa sallim ʿala 'n-nabiyyi 'sh-shakkār.

Yā Qahhār, ṣalli wa sallim ʿala 'n-nabiyyi 'dh-dhakkār.

Yā Wahhāb, ṣalli wa sallim ʿala 'n-nabiyyi 'r-rahhāb.

Yā Razzāq, ṣalli wa sallim ʿala 'n-nabiyyi 'l-jawwād.

Yā Fattāḥ, ṣalli wa sallim ʿala 'n-nabiyyi 'l-awwāh.

Yā ʿAlīm, ṣalli wa sallim ʿala 'n-nabiyyi 'l-ḥalīm.

Yā Qābiḍ, ṣalli wa sallim ʿala 'n-nabiyyi 'l-qāsim.

Yā Bāsiṭ, ṣalli wa sallim ʿala 'n-nabiyyi 'sh-shāhid.

Yā Khāfiḍ, ṣalli wa sallim ʿala 'n-nabiyyi 'l-wāḍiʿ.

Yā Rāfiʿ, ṣalli wa sallim ʿala 'n-nabiyyi 'sh-shāfiʿ.

Yā Mu-ʿizz, ṣalli wa sallim ʿala 'n-nabiyyi 'l-mu-ʿīn.

Yā Mudhill, ṣalli wa sallim ʿala 'n-nabiyyi 'l-muzīl.

Yā Samīʿ, ṣalli wa sallim ʿala 'n-nabiyyi 'sh-shafīʿ.

Yā Baṣīr, ṣalli wa sallim ʿala 'n-nabiyyi 'l-bashīr.

Yā Ḥakam, ṣalli wa sallim ʿala 'n-nabiyyi 'l-akram.

Yā ʿAdl, ṣalli wa sallim ʿala 'n-nabiyyi 'l-badar.

Yā Laṭīf, ṣalli wa sallim ʿala 'n-nabiyyi 'l-ḥanīf.

Yā Khabīr, ṣalli wa sallim ʿala 'n-nabiyyi 'n-nadhīr.

Yā Ḥalīm, ṣalli wa sallim ʿala 'n-nabiyyi 'l-ḥakīm.

Yā ʿAẓīm, ṣalli wa sallim ʿala 'n-nabiyyi 'l-karīm.

Yā Ghafūr, ṣalli wa sallim ʿala 'n-nabiyyi 'ẓ-ẓafūr.

Yā Shakūr, ṣalli wa sallim ʿala 'n-nabiyyi 'ṭ-ṭahūr.

Yā ʿAliyy, ṣalli wa sallim ʿala 'n-nabiyyi 't-taqī.

Yā Kabīr, ṣalli wa sallim ʿala 'n-nabiyyi 'l-ajīr.

Yā Ḥafīẓ, ṣalli wa sallim ʿala 'n-nabiyyi 'l-ʿazīz.

Yā Muqīt, ṣalli wa sallim ʿala 'n-nabiyyi 'l-muqīm.

Yā Ḥasīb, ṣalli wa sallim ʿala 'n-nabiyyi 'n-nasīb.

Yā Jalīl, ṣalli wa sallim ʿala 'n-nabiyyi 'l-khalīl.

Yā Karīm, ṣalli wa sallim ʿala ʾn-nabiyyi ʾr-raḥīm.
Yā Raqīb, ṣalli wa sallim ʿala ʾn-nabiyyi ʾl-ḥabīb.
Yā Mujīb, ṣalli wa sallim ʿala ʾn-nabiyyi ʾl-munīb.
Yā Wāsiʿ, ṣalli wa sallim ʿala ʾn-nabiyyi ʾl-khāshiʿ.
Yā Ḥakīm, ṣalli wa sallim ʿala ʾn-nabiyyi ʾz-za-ʿīm.
Yā Wadūd, ṣalli wa sallim ʿala ʾn-nabiyyi ʾl-hajūd.
Yā Majīd, ṣalli wa sallim ʿala ʾn-nabiyyi ʾs-sa-ʿīd.
Yā Bā-ʿith, ṣalli wa sallim ʿala ʾn-nabiyyi ʾr-rāghib.
Yā Shahīd, ṣalli wa sallim ʿala ʾn-nabiyyi ʾr-rashīd.
Yā Ḥaqq, ṣalli wa sallim ʿala ʾn-nabiyyi ʾl-aṣdaq.
Yā Wakīl, ṣalli wa sallim ʿala ʾn-nabiyyi ʾl-jalīl.
Yā Qawiyy, ṣalli wa sallim ʿala ʾn-nabiyyi ʾṣ-ṣafiyy.
Yā Matīn, ṣalli wa sallim ʿala ʾn-nabiyyi ʾl-amīn.
Yā Waliyy, ṣalli wa sallim ʿala ʾn-nabiyyi ʾl-wafiyy.
Yā Ḥamīd, ṣalli wa sallim ʿala ʾn-nabiyyi ʾs-sadīd.
Yā Muḥṣī, ṣalli wa sallim ʿala ʾn-nabiyyi ʾl-muʿlī.
Yā Mubdiʾ, ṣalli wa sallim ʿala ʾn-nabiyyi ʾl-muqriʾ.
Yā Mu-ʿīd, ṣalli wa sallim ʿala ʾn-nabiyyi ʾl-muḥīd.
Yā Muḥyī, ṣalli wa sallim ʿala ʾn-nabiyyi ʾl-ummiyy.
Yā Mumīt, ṣalli wa sallim ʿala ʾn-nabiyyi ʾl-munīr.
Yā Ḥayy, ṣalli wa sallim ʿala ʾn-nabiyyi ʾl-khayr.

Yā Qayyūm, ṣalli wa sallim ʿala 'n-nabiyyi 'l-manṣūr.
Yā Wājid, ṣalli wa sallim ʿala 'n-nabiyyi 'l-wā-ʿid.
Yā Mājid, ṣalli wa sallim ʿala 'n-nabiyyi 'l-ʿābid.
Yā Wāḥid, ṣalli wa sallim ʿala 'n-nabiyyi 'l-qā'id.
Yā Aḥad, ṣalli wa sallim ʿala 'n-nabiyyi 'l-qamar.
Yā Ṣamad, ṣalli wa sallim ʿala 'n-nabiyyi 'l-bashar.
Yā Qādir, ṣalli wa sallim ʿala 'n-nabiyyi 'shākir.
Yā Muqtadir, ṣalli wa sallim ʿala 'n-nabiyyi 'l-muqtaṣid.
Yā Muqaddim, ṣalli wa sallim ʿala 'n-nabiyyi 'l-muqaddam.
Yā Mu'akhkhir, ṣalli wa sallim ʿala 'n-nabiyyi 'l-mubashshir.
Yā Awwal, ṣalli wa sallim ʿala 'n-nabiyyi 'l-ajmal.
Yā Ākhir, ṣalli wa sallim ʿala 'n-nabiyyi 'dh-dhākir.
Yā Ẓāhir, ṣalli wa sallim ʿala 'n-nabiyyi 'z-zāhir.
Yā Bāṭin, ṣalli wa sallim ʿala 'n-nabiyyi 'l-āmin.
Yā Wālī, ṣalli wa sallim ʿala 'n-nabiyyi 'r-rājī.
Yā Muta-ʿālī, ṣalli wa sallim ʿala 'n-nabiyyi 't-tālī.
Yā Barr, ṣalli wa sallim ʿala 'n-nabiyyi 'l-baḥr.
Yā Tawwāb, ṣalli wa sallim ʿala 'n-nabiyyi 'l-ḥammād.
Yā Muntaqim, ṣalli wa sallim ʿala 'n-nabiyyi 'l-mubtahil.
Yā ʿAfuww, ṣalli wa sallim ʿala 'n-nabiyyi 'l-matluww.
Yā Ra'ūf, ṣalli wa sallim ʿala 'n-nabiyyi 'l-ʿaṭūf.

Yā Mālika 'l-mulk, ṣalli wa sallim ʿala 'n-nabiyyi ḥāmili liwā'i 'l-ḥamd.

Yā Dha 'l-jalāli wa 'l-ikrām, ṣalli wa sallim ʿala 'n-nabiyyi 'l-hudā wa 'l-humām.

Yā Muqsiṭ, ṣalli wa sallim ʿala 'n-nabiyyi 'l-muṣliḥ.

Yā Jāmiʿ, ṣalli wa sallim ʿala 'n-nabiyyi 'l-khāḍiʿ.

Yā Ghaniyy, ṣalli wa sallim ʿala 'n-nabiyyi 's-sakhiyy.

Yā Mughnī, ṣalli wa sallim ʿala 'n-nabiyyi 'l-muhdī.

Yā Māniʿ, ṣalli wa sallim ʿala 'n-nabiyyi 'sh-shāriʿ.

Yā Ḍārr, ṣalli wa sallim ʿala 'n-nabiyyi 'l-kāff.

Yā Nāfiʿ, ṣalli wa sallim ʿala 'n-nabiyyi 'ṣ-ṣāliḥ.

Yā Nūr, ṣalli wa sallim ʿala 'n-nabiyyi 'r-rūḥ.

Yā Hādī, ṣalli wa sallim ʿala 'n-nabiyyi 'sh-shāfī.

Yā Badīʿ, ṣalli wa sallim ʿala 'n-nabiyyi 'l-bahiyy.

Yā Bāqī, ṣalli wa sallim ʿala 'n-nabiyyi 'l-māḥī.

Yā Wārith, ṣalli wa sallim ʿala 'n-nabiyyi 'l-ghālib.

Yā Rashīd, ṣalli wa sallim ʿala 'n-nabiyyi 'n-najīd.

Yā Ṣabūr, ṣalli wa sallim ʿala 'n-nabiyyi 'sh-shakūr.

EXCELLENCE OF INVOKING BLESSINGS

SAKHĀWĪ HAS related a number of accounts related to sending blessings upon Allāh's Most Beloved Messenger ﷺ. To complete the book, a selection is given below.

Ibn Bashkuwāl mentions that it is related from one of the ṣūfis: "I saw a man, known as Misṭaḥ in a dream, after his death. He had been a shameless person while alive. I asked, 'How did Allāh treat you?' He said, 'He forgave me.' I asked, 'On account of what?' He replied, 'I once asked one of the shaykhs of ḥadīth to dictate a *musnad* (traceable) ḥadīth to me. The shaykh invoked blessings upon the Prophet ﷺ and I did likewise, raising my voice as I did so, and when the rest of the assembly heard it, they also invoked blessings [upon him ﷺ]. All of us were forgiven that day.'" (254)

It has been related that Abu 'l-Ḥasan al-Shādhilī (may Allāh have mercy on him) was once in a jungle when some beast confronted him. He was frightened for his safety, but took refuge in invoking blessings upon the Prophet ﷺ. It has been authentically narrated that Allāh will send ten blessings upon whoever sends blessings upon the Prophet ﷺ once, and that *ṣalāt* from Allāh is mercy; whosoever Allāh showers his mercy upon, He suffices for in all his concerns. Abu 'l-Ḥasan al-Shādhilī was thus saved by invoking blessings upon the Prophet ﷺ—may Allāh bless him ﷺ and give him abundant peace. (260)

Abū ʿArūba al-Ḥarrānī used to say, "The *baraka* of ḥadīths lies in the abundance of blessings upon the Prophet ﷺ [they contain] in this world and the favors of Paradise [they are rewarded with] in the Hereafter, if Allāh so wills." (458)

It has been related that Wakīʿ ibn al-Jarrāḥ said: "If it were not for the invocation of blessings in each ḥadīth, I would not narrate ḥadīths to anyone." (458)

It has been reported that Abū Aḥmad al-Zāhid said: "The most blessed, excellent, and beneficial source of knowledge in this world and the Hereafter, after the Book of Allāh Most High, are the ḥadīths of the Messenger ﷺ, because they constitute an abundance of blessings upon him. They are like gardens and orchards. You will find in them all good, piety, and excellence." (458)

Before adjudicating a case, the qāḍī of the Ḥanbalīs in Damascus, Imām Taqī Abu 'l-Faḍl Sulaymān ibn Ḥamza ibn ʿUmar ibn al-

Shaykh Abī ʿUmar, would command: "Invoke blessings upon the Messenger of Allāh ﷺ." After the people had invoked blessings, he would give his judgment. (459)

Muḥammad ibn Ḥimyar relates from Jaʿfar ibn Muḥammad that whoever sends blessings upon the Messenger of Allāh ﷺ in a written work, the angels will invoke blessings on him morning and evening for as long as the name of the Messenger of Allāh ﷺ is in that book. (461)

Numayrī relates that Sufyān ibn ʿUyayna said: "I had a brother with whom I would study ḥadīths. After he passed away, I saw him in a dream. I asked him: 'How has Allāh treated you?' He replied, 'He has forgiven me.' I asked, 'On account of what?' He replied, 'Whenever I wrote ḥadīths and the Messenger of Allāh was mentioned, I would write: "Allāh bless him and give him peace," seeking by it reward. I was thus forgiven because of that.'" (463)

Jaʿfar al-Zaʿfarānī relates that he heard his maternal uncle Ḥasan ibn Muḥammad say: "I saw Aḥmad ibn Ḥanbal in my sleep and he said to me, 'O Abū ʿAlī, if only you could see how the blessings we invoked upon the Messenger ﷺ in our books are shining before us!'" Ibn Bashkuwāl has narrated this ḥadīth. (463)

Ibrāhīm al-Nasafī says: "I saw the Prophet ﷺ in a dream and he seemed to be disheartened by me. I extended my hands and kissed his. I said, 'O Messenger of Allāh, I am one of the scholars of ḥadīth and the People of the Sunna, and I am a stranger?' He ﷺ said, 'When you send blessings on me, why do you not invoke peace on me?' Thereafter, whenever I wrote *ṣalla 'Llāhu ʿalayhi* (May Allāh bless him), I would also write *wa sallam* (and give him peace)." (465)

Jaʿfar ibn ʿAbdillāh relates that he saw Abū Zurʿa in a dream, praying in the heavens with the angels. He asked him: "How have you reached this status?" He replied, "I have written one million ḥadīths with my hand. Whenever I mentioned the Prophet ﷺ I would invoke blessings upon him, and he ﷺ has said, 'Whoever invokes blessings upon me once, Allāh sends ten blessings upon him.'" Ibn ʿAsākir has narrated this account. (465)

It has been narrated that Muzanī said, "I saw [Imām] Shāfiʿī in my dream after his death and asked him: 'How did Allāh treat you?' He said, 'He forgave me because of an invocation of blessing which I made in the book *Al-Risāla*:

اَللّٰهُمَّ صَلِّ عَلٰى مُحَمَّدٍ كُلَّمَا ذَكَرَهُ الذَّاكِرُوْنَ، وَصَلِّ عَلٰى مُحَمَّدٍ كُلَّمَا غَفَلَ عَنْ ذِكْرِهِ الْغَافِلُوْنَ

O Allāh, bless Muḥammad every time those who remember him remember him, and bless him every time those who are neglectful of remembering him neglect to remember him.'" (466)

References

✳

The references cited below are for the fifty ḥadīths of Part One of this manual. Although, the majority of references for the first forty ḥadīths have been cited from *Zād al-Saʿīd* and the independently published manuals, they have also been supplemented by other sources, which are clearly distinguished below. The text of the invocations in this manual is based on that of the independently published manuals taken from *Faḍā'il Durūd Sharīf*. Any differences found in *Zād al-Saʿīd* or any of the original source references have also been mentioned here.

1. Bazzār, Ibn Abī ʿĀṣim, Aḥmad ibn Ḥanbal, Ismāʿīl al-Qāḍī, Ibn Bashkuwāl in *Al-Qurba*, and Ṭabarānī in *Al-Muʿjam al-Ṣaghīr* and *al-Awsaṭ* from Ruwayfiʿ ibn Thābit al-Anṣārī that the Messenger of Allāh ﷺ said, "Whoever reads this, my intercession is necessary for him." Sakhāwī states that some of these chains of transmission are acceptable (*ḥasan*) as Mundhirī has said (see *Al-Qawl al-Badīʿ* 114).
2. Aḥmad from Jābir, with a slight variation.
3. Ibn Ḥibbān from Abū Saʿīd al-Khudrī that the Messenger of Allāh ﷺ said, "Whoever does not possess wealth to spend in charity should include this invocation among his supplications; it will be a source of purification for him."
4. Bayhaqī from ʿAbdullāh ibn Masʿūd.
5. Bukhārī, Muslim, and Nasā'ī from Kaʿb ibn ʿUjra.
6. Muslim, Aḥmad, and Ṭabarānī in his *Al-Muʿjam al-Kabīr* from Kaʿb ibn ʿUjra. Muslim has *Allāhumma bārik* in place of *wa bārik*.

7. Bukhārī and Ibn Māja from Kaʿb ibn ʿUjra.
8. Nasāʾī from Kaʿb ibn ʿUjra, with the addition *wa ʿalā āli Ibrāhīm.*
9. Ṭabarānī in *Al-Muʿjam al-Kabīr* from Kaʿb ibn ʿUjra and Bazzār from Ṭalḥa.
10. Abū Dāwūd from Kaʿb ibn ʿUjra.
11. Muslim, Abū Dāwūd, and Tirmidhī from Abū Masʿūd al-Anṣārī.
12. Bukhārī, Abū Dāwūd, Nasāʾī, and Ibn Māja from Abū Ḥumayd al-Sāʿidī.
13. Bukhārī and Muslim from Abū Ḥumayd al-Sāʿidī.
14. Abū Dāwūd from Abū Hurayra that the Messenger of Allāh said, "Whoever desires that they be given a full reward when invoking blessings on my household should read this invocation."
15. Bukhārī in *Al-Adab al-Mufrad* and Ṭabarī in *Tahdhīb al-Āthār* from Abū Hurayra that the Messenger of Allāh said, "Whoever makes these invocations, I will be a witness for him and intercede for him."
16. Khayrūbarī in *Kitāb al-Ṣalāt* from ʿAlī (*Zād al-Saʿīd*). Bayhaqī in *Shuʿab al-Īmān* from ʿAlī and Ḥākim in *ʿUlūm al-Ḥadīth.* This ḥadīth is also considered *musalsal bi ʾl-ʿadd,* and has been recorded in the *musalsalāt* collections (narrations with a successively corroborated chain in which an additional feature is mentioned). ʿAlī narrates that the Messenger of Allāh counted on my fingers and said, "Jibrīl counted on my fingers, and said, 'This is the way I have descended with them [i.e., the five invocations] from the Lord of Majesty, Most Mighty, Most Majestic.'" Sakhāwī states that Ibn Bashkuwāl has transmitted this in *Al-Qurba,* Ibn Masdī in his *Musalsalāt,* Qāḍī ʿIyāḍ in *Al-Shifāʾ,* Hannād al-Nasafī, and others (*Al-Qawl al-Badīʿ* 107–108). See also *Kanz al-ʿUmmāl,* #3990, 1:215.
17. Majd al-Aʾimma al-Tarjumānī from ʿAlī, Ibn Masʿūd, and Jābir (*Zād al-Saʿīd*). A narration very similar to this is also found in the *Mustadrak* of Ḥākim; it does not contain the words *wa sallim* in the second sentence nor *fī ʾl-ʿālamīn* in the last sentence, although these words are found as parts of other narrations. See also *Al-Qawl al-Badīʿ* 105.

18. Bukhārī from Kaᶜb ibn ᶜUjra.
19. Bukhārī, Nasāʾī, Ibn Māja, Aḥmad, Bayhaqī, and Ibn Abī ᶜĀṣim from Abū Saᶜīd al-Khudrī (*Al-Qawl al-Badīᶜ* 104).
20. Nasāʾī from Abū Masᶜūd in *Al-Sunan al-Kubrā*.
21. Sakhāwī mentions in *Al-Qawl al-Badīᶜ* that Abū ᶜĀṣim relates in one of his collections that the Messenger of Allāh said, "Whoever makes this invocation seven times for seven Fridays my intercession will be necessary for him. There is a slight variation in the wording of the invocation in ᶜAwwāma's edition of *Al-Qawl al-Badīᶜ* (125).
22. Aḥmad, Ḥākim, and Bayhaqī in his *Sunan* from ᶜAbdullāh ibn Masᶜūd.
23. Dāraquṭnī from ᶜAbdullāh ibn Masᶜūd.
24. Aḥmad from Burayda.
25. Nasāʾī from Ḥusayn ibn ᶜAlī with *Muḥammad* in place of *al-Ummiyy*.
26. Bukhārī and Nasāʾī from ᶜAbdullāh ibn Masᶜūd.
27. Muslim and Nasāʾī from Abū Mūsā al-Ashᶜarī. *Zād al-Saᶜīd* has *li 'Llāh* after *Al-Taḥiyyāt* as narrated by Nasāʾī in another version.
28. Nasāʾī from Abū Mūsā al-Ashᶜarī.
29. Nasāʾī from ᶜAbdullāh ibn ᶜAbbās.
30. Nasāʾī from Jābir.
31. Mālik in his *Muwaṭṭā* and Ḥākim in his *Mustadrak* from ᶜUmar ibn al-Khaṭṭāb. This narration is *mawqūf*.
32. Ṭabarānī in *Al-Muᶜjam al-Awsaṭ* and *al-Kabīr* from ᶜAbdullāh ibn al-Zubayr.
33. Abū Dāwūd and Ṭabarānī in *Al-Muᶜjam al-Kabīr* from Samura ibn Jundub to *al-mulku li 'Llāh*. Shaykh Thānawī has added the additional words, saying that the narrator most likely shortened it for the sake of brevity. According to the narration in Ṭabarānī the Prophet said, "Then invoke peace on the Prophet ..."
34. Mālik in his *Muwaṭṭā* that ᶜAbdullāh ibn ᶜUmar used to make this invocation for the *tashahhud*. Shaykh Thānawī states that although this invocation has not been related directly from the Messenger of Allāh, it can be surmised as

having been acquired from him ﷺ by Ibn ʿUmar ؓ on the basis that remembrances are not made part of the prayer through one's personal opinion.

35. Mālik in his *Muwaṭṭā* that ʿĀ'isha ؓ used to recite this invocation.
36. Mālik in his *Muwaṭṭā* that ʿĀ'isha ؓ used to recite this invocation.
37. Ibn Ḥibbān from Abū Mūsā al-Ashʿarī ؓ.
38. Abū Dāwūd from ʿAbdullāh ibn ʿUmar ؓ.
39. Muslim and Ibn Ḥibbān from ʿAbdullāh ibn ʿAbbās ؓ. *Zād al-Saʿīd* has *Wa ashhadu anna Muḥammadan ʿabduhū wa rasūluh* at the end as is narrated by Ibn Māja.
40. Ibn Māja in his *Sunan* and Ibn Abī Shayba in his *Muṣannaf* from Fāṭima ؓ.
41. Abu 'l-Qāsim al-Sabtī al-ʿAzafī in *Al-Durr al-Munaẓẓam fī 'l-Mawlid al-Muʿaẓẓam* (*Al-Qawl al-Badīʿ* 116).
42. Ṭabarānī and Daylamī from ʿAbdullāh ibn ʿUmar ؓ (*Al-Qawl al-Badīʿ* 447, *Dharīʿat al-Wuṣūl* 46).
43. Numayrī and Ibn Bashkuwāl from Abu 'l-Ḥasan ibn al-Karkhī, a companion of Maʿrūf al-Karkhī, that the latter would make this invocation (*Al-Qawl al-Badīʿ* 123, *Dharīʿat al-Wuṣūl* 103).
44. *Al-Qawl al-Badīʿ* 130 and *Dharīʿat al-Wuṣūl* 68.
45. ʿAbd ibn Ḥumayd in his *Musnad*, ʿAbd al-Razzāq, and Ismāʿīl al-Qāḍī with a strong and authenticated chain from Ibn ʿAbbās ؓ (*Al-Qawl al-Badīʿ* 122, *Dharīʿat al-Wuṣūl* 68).
46. Bayhaqī relates that Imām Shāfiʿī was seen in a dream and he was asked, "How did Allāh treat you?" He responded, "Allāh forgave me." So he was asked, "On account of what?" He said, "Five prayers through which I used to invoke blessings on the Messenger of Allāh ﷺ." He was asked what they were and he read these five (*Al-Qawl al-Badīʿ* 467, *Dharīʿat al-Wuṣūl* 113, 159).
47. Daylamī in *Musnad al-Firdaws* with a weak chain from ʿAbdullāh ibn ʿAbbās ؓ. Muḥammad ʿAwwāma the editor of *Al-Qawl al-Badīʿ* states that this supplication has been related from Abū Hurayra ؓ (*Al-Qawl al-Badīʿ* 123). Abu 'l-Fatḥ al-Maqdisī states in *Kitāb al-Adʿiyyāt al-Mustajābāt* quoting from Ibn ʿAbbās ؓ

that the Messenger of Allāh ﷺ said that the one who makes this invocation, Allāh will remove the grief he is engulfed in. In his *Adhkār,* Imām Suyūṭī therefore included this invocation among those to be read at times of grief (*Dharīʿat al-Wuṣūl* 47–49).

48. Numayrī has related that Ḥasan al-Baṣrī used to make this invocation (*Al-Qawl al-Badīʿ* 122, *Dharīʿat al-Wuṣūl* 96).
49. Fākihānī has related this invocation in *Al-Fajr al-Munīr* from Shaykh Ṣāliḥ Mūsā al-Ḍarīr. Majd al-Dīn al-Fayrūzābādī has also transmitted it through his chain and has related after it from Ḥasan ibn ʿAlī al-Aswānī that whoever makes this invocation one thousand times for any matter of concern or need, or in a calamity, Allāh will relieve them of the problem and the person will attain his objective (*Al-Qawl al-Badīʿ* 415–416, *Dharīʿat al-Wuṣūl* 73). This invocation has also been called *Ṣalāt Tunjīnā.*
50. Qāḍī ʿIyāḍ in *Al-Shifā'* from ʿAlī ﷺ (*Al-Qawl al-Badīʿ* 121).

BIBLIOGRAPHY

✳

al-Fayrūzābādī, Majd al-Dīn Muḥammad ibn Ya'qūb. *Al-Qāmūs al-Muḥīṭ*. Ed. Yūsuf al-Shaykh Muḥammad al-Baqā'ī. Beirut: Dār al-Fikr, 1415/1995.

al-Ghazālī, Abū Ḥāmid. *Al-Ghazali: The Ninety Nine Beautiful Names of God* [an English translation with notes of Ghazālī's *Al-Maqṣad al-Asnā fī Sharḥ Asmā' Allāh al-Ḥusnā* by David B. Burrell and Nazih Dahler]. Reprint. Cambridge: Islamic Text Society, 1415/1995.

Ibn Manẓūr. *Lisān al-'Arab*. Ed. Amīn Muḥammad 'Abd al-Wahhāb and Muḥammad al-Ṣādiq al-'Abīdī. 18 vols. Beirut: Dār Iḥyā' al-Turāth al-'Arabī and Mu'assasat al-Tārikh al-'Arabī, 1419/1999.

Islamul Haq. *Ṣalāt wa Salām kā Maqbūl Waẓīfa*. Holcombe Bury: Darul Uloom, n.d.

Lane, E. W. *Arabic-English Lexicon*. Cambridge: Islamic Text Society, 1404/1984.

Mia, Ibrahim A.R. *Salat and Salaam Upon the Best of Creations* (*Al-Ṣalāt wa 'l-Salām 'alā Khayr al-Anām*). Lenasia: Darun Nashr Rahmaniyyah, n.d.

Motala, Yusuf ibn Sulayman. *Ṣalāt wa Salām 'alā Sayyid al-Anām bi 'l-Asmā' al-Ilāhiyya wa 'l-Alqāb al-Nabawiyya*. Lahore: Khānqāh Iḥsāniyya Imdādiyya Chistiyya, n.d.

———. [A translation of *Ṣalāt wa Salām* in English by Khalil Ahmed Kazi]. Karachi: Haji Moosa Desai & Khatija Bai Trust, n.d.

al-Nawawī, Muḥy al-Dīn Abū Zakariyya Yaḥyā ibn Sharaf. *Al-Adhkār al-Muntakhab min Kalām Sayyid al-Abrār*. Ed. Muḥammad Rājī ibn Ḥasan Kannās. Beirut and Halab: Dār al-Sharq al-ʿArabī, n.d.

Nuʿmānī, Muḥammad Manẓūr. *Maʿārif al-Ḥadīth*. 7 vols. in 3. Lahore: ʿUmar Fārūq Academy, n.d.

al-Patnī, Muḥammad ibn Ṭāhir ibn ʿAlī al-Gujarātī al-Hindī. *Majmaʿ Biḥār al-Anwār*. Third Edition. Madina: Maktaba Dār al-Īmān, 1415/1994.

al-Sakhāwī, Muḥammad ibn ʿAbd al-Raḥmān. *Al-Qawl al-Badīʿ fi 'l-Ṣalāt ʿala 'l-Ḥabīb al-Shafīʿ*. Ed. Muḥammad ʿAwwāma. First Edition. Beirut: Mu'assasat al-Rayyān, 1422/2002.

Sindhī, Makhdūm Muḥammad Hāshim. *Dharīʿat al-Wuṣūl ilā Janāb al-Rasūl* ﷺ [a translation of Sindhī' *Dharīʿat al-Wuṣūl* by Yūsuf Ludhyānwī from Persian into Urdu]. Karachi: Maktaba Bayyināt, n.d.

Thānawī, Muḥammad Ashraf ʿAlī. *Zād al-Saʿīd* (or *Faḍā'il Durūd wa Salām*). Ed. Meherbān ʿAlī Barotawī. Bombay: Maktaba Ashrafiyya, n.d.

Wehr, Hans. *A Dictionary of Modern Written Arabic*. Ed. J Milton Cowan. Reprint. Beirut: Librarie Du Liban. 1395/1976.

Biographies

✳

Imām Shams al-Dīn Muḥammad ibn ʿAbd al-Raḥmān al-Sakhāwī, born in 831/1427 in Cairo, was one of the foremost students of Shaykh al-Islām Aḥmad ibn Ḥajar al-ʿAsqalānī (d. 852/1449). Sakhāwī was a great jurist, historian, and a ḥadīth master. Among his numerous works are *Al-Maqaṣid al-Ḥasana* and *Al-Qawl al-Badīʿ fi 'l-Ṣalāt ʿala 'l-Ḥabīb al-Shafīʿ*; the latter is considered one of the greatest and most comprehensible works written on the subject of invoking blessings upon Allāh's Messenger ﷺ. He died in 902/1496.

ʿAllāma Makhdūm Muḥammad Hāshim Sindhī, born in 1104/1692, was a contemporary of Shāh Walī Allāh, the great ḥadīth scholar of Delhi, and was considered the Shāh Walī Allāh of the Sindh province. He was a leading imām of the Islamic sciences of *tafsīr*, ḥadīth, *fiqh*, *uṣūl*, theology, *taṣawwuf*, history, Arabic, and poetry. He was also exemplary in his piety, asceticism, and *taqwā*. He was fluent in Arabic, Persian, and Sindhi, and was blessed with *baraka* in his time and thus wrote on many subjects. Despite producing an immense body of work, he maintained his standard of excellence throughout. He died in 1174/1760.

Mawlānā Ashraf ʿAlī Thānawī, referred to by many as Ḥakīm al-Umma (Spiritual Physician of the Muslim Umma), was born in 1280/1863 in India, and was a towering figure of Islamic revival and reawakening of South Asia in the twentieth century. He was the most eminent religious figure of his time, a prolific author, and believed to be one of the greatest scholars and ṣūfīs of modern India. A great writer, a spiritual jurist, an intellectual sage, and a fortifier of Islamic tradition, he passed away in 1362/1943.

SHAYKH YUSUF IBN SULAYMAN MOTALA, considered today by many as one of the greatest visionaries and preservers of the faith in the UK, was born 1366/1946 in Gujarat, India. He began his studies at Jamea Husainia in Rander, Gujarat and graduated from the renowned Mazahir Uloom in Saharanpur. He became one of the senior disciples of the late Shaykh al-Ḥadīth Mawlānā Muḥammad Zakariyya Kāndhlawī. In 1387/1968, upon the instructions of his Shaykh, he immigrated to England to set up what has been heralded as the first Islamic seminary in the West, Darul Uloom Al-Arabiyyah Al-Islamiyyah in Holcombe, Bury, Lancashire. This seminary, established in 1392/1973, has succeeded in producing hundreds of scholars and alumni, who after studying under the Shaykh, are spread around the globe teaching and serving the religion of Allāh. Shaykh Yusuf is also the founder and patron of numerous other Islamic institutions around the world, and is the author of several books. His *Obedience to the Messenger* (*Iṭāʿat al-Rasūl*) is particularly noteworthy in that his love and respect for the Messenger of Allāh ﷺ can be seen deeply ingrained in every word in it. He currently holds the position as the rector and senior lecturer of ḥadīth at the seminary, and has been teaching the *Ṣaḥīḥ al-Bukhārī* and other works for a number of years, along with fulfilling his position as a spiritual teacher to many.

Our Publications

Prayers for Forgiveness
The Path to Perfection
Sufism & Good Character
The Differences of the Imāms
Provisions for the Seekers
Ghazālī's The Beginning of Guidance (*Bidāyat al-Hidāya*)
Saviours of Islamic Spirit (*Tārīkh-i Daʿwat wa ʿAẓīmat*)
Reflections of Pearls
Fiqh al-Imam: Key Proofs in Hanafi Fiqh
The Islamic Laws of Animal Slaughter
Absolute Essentials of Islam
Ṣalāt & Salām: A Manual of Blessings on Allāh's Beloved
Imām Abū Ḥanīfa's *Al-Fiqh al-Akbar* Explained
Ascent to Felicity (*Marāqī 'l-Saʿādāt*)
The Book of Wisdoms (*Ikmāl al-Shiyam*)
Birth Control & Abortion in Islam
The Shāfiʿī Manual of Purity, Prayer & Fasting
Al-Ḥizb al-Aʿẓam (The Supreme Daily Remembrance)

www.whitethreadpress.com